Irving Babbitt, born in Dayton, Ohio, in 1865, graduated from Harvard with honors in 1889. He studied Sanskrit language and Indian philosophy under Sylvain Lévi at the École des Hautes Études, Paris, and then returned to Harvard for his M.A. (1893). In 1894 he became a French teacher at Harvard and was made a full professor in 1912; he remained there until his death in 1933. Despite his life-long interest in the language and thought of the East, he never visited the Orient, though his wife was born and brought up in China. During his last illness, he worked on *The Dhammapada*, but never completed the notes. The book was published posthumously.

Babbitt published seven books: *Literature and the American College: Essays in the Defense of the Humanities* (1908); *The New Laokoon* (1910); *The Masters of Modern French Criticism* (1912); *Rousseau and Romanticism* (1919); *Democracy and Leadership* (1924); *On Being Creative and Other Essays* (1932); and *The Dhammapada* (1936). A second posthumous volume, *Spanish Character and Other Essays*, appeared in 1940.

With Paul Elmer More, Babbitt was a leading exponent of what came to be called the "New Humanism," which still has many echoes in present-day criticism. Among those who studied under and were strongly influenced by Babbitt were T. S. Eliot, Norman Foerster, Van Wyck Brooks, Austin Warren, and Theodore Spencer; other students less directly his disciples were Walter Lippmann, Gilbert Seldes, Newton Arvin, Harry Levin, Granville Hicks, and Crane Brinton.

'This is not a doctrine for the sluggard but for the man who puts forth virile effort.'
— *Anguttara-Nikāya*, IV, p. 232.

'The Tathāgata has no theories.'
— *Majjhima-Nikāya*, I, p. 486.

THE DHAMMAPADA

Translated from the Pāli
with an Essay
on Buddha and the Occident

BY

IRVING BABBITT

A NEW DIRECTIONS PAPERBOOK

Originally published by Oxford University Press, New York.
First published as New Directions Paperbook 188 in 1965.

Published simultaneously in Canada by Penguin Books Canada Limited.

Library of Congress Catalog Card Number 64-23655
ISBN: 0-8112-0004-3

Manufactured in the United States of America
New Directions books are printed on acid-free paper.

FOURTEENTH PRINTING

New Directions Books are published for James Laughlin
by New Directions Publishing Corporation,
80 Eighth Avenue, New York 10011

CONTENTS

NOTE ON THE DHAMMAPADA

THE word Dhammapada may perhaps best be rendered Path of Virtue, provided one keep in mind that virtue means practically the Buddhist Law or Norm. According to the usual arrangement it appears as the tenth division of the Khuddaka-nikaya, itself the fifth division of the Suttapitaka, the second of the 'three baskets' (Ti-pitaka) that constitute the Buddhist Canon as preserved by the Theravādins or School of the Elders. The Canon thus constituted is accepted today in Ceylon, Burma, Siam, etc., in short in the lands where the form of Buddhism known as the Small Vehicle (Hīnayāna) prevails. The language of the Ti-pitaka is Pāli, supposed to have been the dialect spoken in the province of Magadha in northeastern India about the sixth century before Christ. Pāli is a sort of softened Sanskrit ; its relation to Sanskrit has indeed been compared to that of Italian to Latin. Nirvāna, for example, becomes nibbāna, bhikshu (monk) bhikkhu, etc. I have not hesitated to use the Sanskrit instead of the Pāli form when it happens to be more familiar to the Western reader.

Some portions of the Ti-pitaka are in prose, some in verse, and others in a mingling of the two. The Dhammapada is entirely in verse. The four hundred and twenty-three stanzas of which it is composed are in various metres, all related to the verse form in Sanskrit known as the çloka.

The relation of the Pāli Canon in its present form to

the original teaching of Buddha, on the one hand, and, on the other, to the scriptures of other schools of Buddhism in Sanskrit, Thibetan, Chinese, etc., raises questions of extreme complexity. Anyone who seeks fuller information regarding these questions may consult with profit the volume by E. J. Thomas, *The Life of Buddha as Legend and History*. The attitude of Mr. Thomas towards Buddhism reminds one of that of the 'higher critics' towards Christianity. It is well to remember in regard to this attitude that it is often as extreme in its way as the uncritical acquiescence of the orthodox Buddhist or Christian in tradition. Practically all scholars who have earned the right to have an opinion now admit, not only that Buddha actually lived, but that he taught the four noble truths. This is to admit a great deal, for the Ti-pitaka is in large measure simply a dialectical development of these truths. The fact is that one cannot read long in the Pāli records without getting the impression of a definite doctrine and a definite personality. For the personality of Buddha, which seems to many even more impressive than the doctrine, one needs to turn from the Dhammapada to other portions of the Canon, especially perhaps to certain Suttas of the Dīgha-nikāya. Doctrinally, however, there is no reason to doubt that most of the verses of the Dhammapada, even if they do not reproduce the *ipsissima verba* of Buddha, are true to the spirit of his teaching. The Buddhists themselves recommend the collection for those who wish to get an initiation into the faith that is sound as far as it goes.

The present translation is a revision of the one first published by Max Müller in 1870 and later included in the tenth volume of the *Sacred Books of the East* (first edition, 1881 ; second edition, 1898). I have aimed to depart as little as possible from the literal sense, even though this literalness has involved at times some sacrifice of elegance. It should be added that there is a formidable obstacle in the way of any rendering of a Buddhist text that will not be misleading, and that is the existence of numerous general terms in Pāli that have no exact equivalent in English or any other Occidental language. One way of meeting the difficulty would have been to append to the present translation short essays on such terms as *dhamma, samkhāra, khanda, āsava, tanhā, nāma-rūpa* and the like. My decision not to write these essays is due to the conviction that the only way to grasp fully the meaning of these terms is to gain a wider acquaintance with the Pāli Canon than that afforded by the Dhammapada. Even so it is difficult, for reasons which I have tried to state in "Buddha and the Occident," for the Occidental, even the Occidental who has read the texts widely in the original, to catch life from the Buddhist angle.

In revising Max Müller's version I have consulted with profit the text (with Latin translation) by Fausböll (first edition, 1855 ; second revised edition, 1900) ; and the edition of the Pāli text published by the Pāli Text Society and edited by Suriyagoda Sumangala Thera (1914). I have consulted the German verse translation by K. E. Neumann (1893), the English verse translation by F. L. Woodward (1921), and the prose rendering by W. D. C. Wagiswara and K. J. Saunders in the Wisdom of the East Series (1920). I have also profited by the portions of the *Dhammapada Commentary* translated by E. W. Burlingame for the Harvard Oriental Series (three volumes, 1921).

Finally I wish to express my obligations to my old teachers, Sylvain Lévi, Professor of Sanskrit at the Collège de France, and to Charles Rockwell Lanman, Professor emeritus of Sanskrit at Harvard University.

I scarcely need add that they are not to be held in the least responsible for my interpretation of Buddhism and still less for any inaccuracies into which I may have fallen through an inadequate knowledge of Pāli.

THE DHAMMAPADA

CHAPTER I

1. All that we are is the result of what we have thought : it is founded on our thoughts, it is made up of our thoughts. If a man speaks or acts with an evil thought, pain follows him, as the wheel follows the foot of the ox that draws the wagon.

2. All that we are is the result of what we have thought : it is founded on our thoughts, it is made up of our thoughts. If a man speaks or acts with a pure thought, happiness follows him, like a shadow that never leaves him.

3. 'He abused me, he beat me, he defeated me, he robbed me,' — in those who harbour such thoughts hatred will never cease.

4. 'He abused me, he beat me, he defeated me, he robbed me,' — in those who do not harbour such thoughts hatred will cease.

5. For never does hatred cease by hatred here below : hatred ceases by love ; this is an eternal law.

6. The world does not know that we must all come to an end here ; but those who know, their quarrels cease at once.

7. He who lives looking for pleasures only, his senses uncontrolled, immoderate in his food, idle and weak, him Māra (the tempter) will surely overthrow, as the wind throws down a weak tree.

8. He who lives without looking for pleasures, his senses well controlled, moderate in his food, faithful and strong, him Māra will certainly not overthrow, any more than the wind throws down a rock mountain.

9. He who wishes to put on the yellow robe though still impure and disregardful of temperance and truth is unworthy of the yellow robe.

10. But whoever has cleansed himself from impurity, is well-grounded in all virtues, and regards also temperance and truth, is indeed worthy of the yellow robe.

11. They who imagine truth in untruth, and see untruth in truth, never arrive at truth, but follow vain desires.

12. They who know truth in truth and untruth in untruth, arrive at truth and follow true desires.

13. As rain breaks through an ill-thatched house, lust breaks through an ill-trained mind.

14. As rain does not break through a well-thatched house, lust will not break through a well-trained mind.

15. The evil-doer mourns in this world and he mourns in the next; he mourns in both. He mourns and suffers when he sees the evil of his own work.

16. The virtuous man delights in this world, and he delights in the next; he delights in both. He delights and rejoices when he sees the purity of his own work.

17. The evil-doer suffers in this world and he suffers in the next; he suffers in both. He suffers when he thinks of the evil he has done : he suffers even more when he has gone in the evil path (to hell).

18. The virtuous man is happy in this world and he is happy in the next; he is happy in both. He is happy when he thinks of the good he has done. He is even happier when he has gone on the good path (to heaven).

19. The slothful man even if he can recite many sacred verses, but does not act accordingly, has no share in the priesthood, but is like a cowherd counting another's kine.

20. If a man can recite but few sacred verses but is a follower of the Law, and, having forsaken lust and ill-will and delusion, possesses true knowledge and serenity of mind, he, clinging to nothing in this world or that to come, has indeed a share in the priesthood.

CHAPTER II

21. Earnestness is the path of immortality, thoughtlessness the path of death. Those who are earnest do not die, those who are thoughtless are as if dead already.

22. Those who, having understood this clearly, are advanced in earnestness, delight therein, rejoicing in the knowledge of the Ariyas (the elect).

23. These wise people, meditative, persevering, always possessed of strong powers, attain to Nirvāna, the highest happiness.

24. If a man is earnest and exerts himself, if he is ever-mindful, if his deeds are pure, if he acts with consideration and restraint and lives according to the Law, — then his glory will increase.

25. By rousing himself, by earnestness, by temperance and self-control, the wise man may make for himself an island which no flood can overwhelm.

26. Senseless and foolish folk fall into sloth. The wise man guards earnestness as his best treasure.

27. Follow not after vanity, nor after the enjoyment of love and lust. He who is earnest and meditative obtains ample joy.

28. When the learned man drives away vanity by earnestness, he, the wise, climbing the terraced heights of wisdom, looks down upon the fools, free from sorrow he looks upon the sorrowing crowd, as one that

6

stands on a mountain looks down upon them that stand upon the plain.

29. Earnest among the slothful, awake among the sleepers, the wise man advances like a racer, leaving behind the hack.

30. By earnestness did Maghavan (Indra) rise to the lordship of the gods. People praise earnestness ; thoughtlessness is always blamed.

31. A mendicant who delights in earnestness, who looks with fear on thoughtlessness, advances like a fire, burning all his fetters both great and small.

32. A mendicant who delights in earnestness, who looks with fear on thoughtlessness, cannot fall away (from his perfect state) — he is close upon Nirvāna.

CHAPTER III

33. As a fletcher makes straight his arrow, a wise man makes straight his trembling and unsteady thought, which is difficult to guard, difficult to hold back.

34. As a fish taken from his watery home and thrown on the dry ground, our thought quivers all over in its effort to escape the dominion of Māra (the tempter).

35. It is good to tame the mind, which is difficult to hold in and flighty, rushing wherever it listeth ; a tamed mind brings happiness.

36. Let the wise man guard his thoughts which are difficult to perceive, very artful and rushing wherever they list : thoughts well guarded bring happiness.

37. Those who bridle their mind which travels far, moves about alone, is without a body, and hides in the chamber (of the heart), are freed from the bonds of Māra (the tempter).

38. If a man's thoughts are unsteady, if he does not know the true Law, his knowledge will never be perfect.

39. If a man's thoughts are free from lust, if his mind is not perplexed, if he has renounced merit and demerit, then there is no fear for him while he is watchful.

40. Knowing that this body is (fragile) like a jar, and making this thought firm like a fortress, one should attack Māra (the tempter) with the weapon of knowledge, one should watch him when conquered and should never falter.

41. Before long, alas ! this body will lie on the ground,

despised, bereft of consciousness, like a useless log.

42. Whatever a hater may do to a hater, or an enemy to an enemy, a wrongly-directed mind will do us greater mischief.

43. Not a mother, not a father will do so much, nor any other relative ; a well-directed mind will do us greater service.

CHAPTER IV

FLOWERS

44. Who shall overcome this Earth, and the world of Yama (the lord of the departed), and the world of the gods? Who shall find out the well-taught path of virtue, even as a clever (garland weaver) picks out the (right) flower?

45. The disciple will overcome the Earth, and the world of Yama, and the world of the gods. The disciple will find out the well-taught path of virtue, even as a clever (garland-weaver) picks out the right flower.

46. He who knows that this body is like froth and has learned that it is as unsubstantial as a mirage, will break the flower-tipped arrow of Māra, and never see the King of death.

47. Death carries off a man who is gathering flowers and whose mind is distracted, as a flood carries off a sleeping village.

48. Death overpowers a man who is gathering flowers, and whose mind is distracted, before he is satiated in his pleasures.

49. As the bee collects nectar and departs without injuring the flower or its colour or scent, so let a sage go about a village.

50. Not the perversities of others, not what they have done or left undone should a sage take notice of.

51. Like a beautiful flower, full of colour, but without scent, are the fair but fruitless words of him who does not act accordingly.

52. Like a beautiful flower, full of colour and full of scent, are the pure and fruitful words of him who acts accordingly.

53. Even as one may make many kinds of wreaths from a heap of flowers, so should one born to the mortal lot, perform good deeds manifold.

54. The scent of flowers does not travel against the wind, nor that of sandal-wood, or of Tagara and Mallikā flowers ; but the fragrance of good people travels even against the wind ; a good man pervades every place.

55. Sandal-wood or Tagara, a lotus-flower or a Vassiki, among these sorts of perfumes the perfume of virtue is preëminent.

56. Mean is the scent that comes from Tagara and sandal-wood ; — the perfume of those who possess virtue rises up to the gods as the highest.

57. Of the people thus excellently virtuous, abiding in earnestness and emancipated through true knowledge, Māra (the tempter) never finds the way.

58, 59. As on a heap of rubbish cast upon the highway the lotus will grow full of sweet perfume and delight, thus the disciple of the truly enlightened Buddha shines forth by his knowledge among those who are like rubbish, among the people who walk in darkness.

CHAPTER V

60. Long is the night to him who is awake ; long is a league to him who is tired ; long is the round of rebirth to the foolish who do not know the true Law.

61. If a traveller does not meet with one who is his better or his equal, let him keep firmly to his solitary journey ; there is no companionship with a fool.

62. 'These sons belong to me, and this wealth belongs to me,' with such thoughts a fool is tormented. He himself does not belong to himself ; how much less sons and wealth ?

63. The fool who knows his foolishness is wise at least so far. But a fool who thinks himself wise, he is called a fool indeed.

64. If a fool be associated with a wise man even all his life, he will perceive the truth as little as a spoon perceives the taste of soup.

65. If an intelligent man be associated for one minute only with a wise man, he will soon perceive the truth, as the tongue perceives the taste of soup.

66. Fools of little understanding are their own greatest enemies, for they do evil deeds which must bear bitter fruits.

67. That deed is not well done of which a man must repent, and the reward of which he receives crying and with a tearful face.

68. No, that deed is well done of which a man does not repent and the reward of which he receives gladly and cheerfully.

69. As long as the evil deed done does not bear fruit, the fool thinks it is like honey ; but when it ripens, then the fool suffers grief.

70. Let a fool month after month eat his food (like an ascetic) with the tip of a blade of Kusha grass, yet is he not worth the sixteenth part of those who have well-weighed the Law.

71. An evil deed like newly-drawn milk does not turn at once; smouldering like fire covered with ashes, it follows the fool.

72. The knowledge that a fool acquires, so far from profiting him, destroys his good fortune, nay, it cleaves his head.

73. Let the fool wish for a false reputation, for precedence among the monks, for lordship in the monasteries, for honour among other people.

74. 'May both laymen and those who have left the world think that this is done by me ; may they be subject to me in everything which is to be done or is not to be done': thus is the mind of the fool, and his desire and pride increase.

75. One is the road that leads to wealth, another the road that leads to Nirvāna ; if the monk, the disciple of Buddha, has learnt this he will not delight in the praise of men, he will strive after separation from the world.

CHAPTER VI

THE WISE MAN

76. If you see an intelligent man who detects faults and blames what is blame-worthy, follow that wise man as though he were a revealer of (hidden) treasures.

77. Let him admonish, let him teach, let him forbid what is improper ! — he will be beloved of the good, by the bad he will be hated.

78. Do not have evil-doers for friends, do not have low people for friends : have virtuous people for friends, have for friends the best of men.

79. He who drinks in the Law lives happily with a serene mind ; the wise man ever rejoices in the Law as taught by the elect (Ariyas).

80. Irrigators guide the water (wherever they like) ; fletchers bend the arrow ; carpenters bend a log of wood ; wise people fashion themselves.

81. As a solid rock is not shaken by the wind, wise people falter not amidst blame and praise.

82. Wise people, after they have listened to the laws, become serene like a deep, clear and still lake.

83. Good people walk on, whatever befall ; the good do not prattle, longing for pleasure ; whether touched by happiness or sorrow, wise people never appear elated or depressed.

84. If, whether for his own sake or for the sake of others, a man wishes neither for a son nor for wealth, nor for lordship, and if he does not wish for his own success by unfair means, then he is good, wise and upright.

85. Few are there among men who arrive at the other shore (become Arhats) ; the other people here merely run up and down the shore.

86. But those who, when the Law has been well preached to them, follow the Law, will reach the further shore of the dominion of death, hard to traverse though it be.

87, 88. A wise man should leave the way of darkness and follow the way of light. After going from his home to the houseless state, he should in his retirement look for enjoyment where enjoyment is hard to find. Leaving all pleasure behind, and calling nothing his own, the wise man should purge himself from all the impurities of the heart.

89. Those whose minds are well-grounded in the (seven) elements of knowledge, who rejoice in the renunciation of affections and in freedom from attachment, whose evil proclivities have been overcome and who are full of light, are completely liberated even in this world.

CHAPTER VII

90. There is no suffering for him who has finished his journey, and abandoned grief, who has freed himself on all sides, and thrown off all fetters.

91. They depart with their thoughts well-collected, they do not delight in an abode ; like swans who have left their lake, they leave their house and home.

92. Men who have laid up no store, who live on recognized food, who have perceived void and unconditional freedom, their path is difficult to understand, like that of birds in the air.

93. He whose appetites are stilled, who is moderate in food, who has perceived void and unconditional freedom, his path is difficult to understand like that of birds in the air.

94. The gods even envy him whose senses like horses well broken in by the driver, have been subdued, who is free from pride, and free from evil propensities.

95. Such a man who does his duty is tolerant like the earth, like a stone set in a threshold ; he is like a lake without mud ; no new births are in store for him.

96. His thought is quiet, quiet are his words and deed, when he has obtained freedom by true knowledge, when he has thus become a quiet man.

97. The man who is free from credulity, but knows the uncreated, who has cut all ties, removed all temptations, renounced all desires, he is the greatest of men.

98. In a hamlet or in a forest, on the sea or on the dry

land, wherever venerable persons (Arhats) dwell, that place is delightful.

99. Forests are delightful ; where the worldly find no delight, there the passionless will find delight, for they look not for pleasures.

CHAPTER VIII

100. Even though a speech be composed of a thousand words, but words without sense, one word of sense is better, which if a man hears he becomes quiet.

101. Even though a stanza be composed of a thousand words but words without sense, one word of a stanza is better which if a man hears, he becomes quiet.

102. Though a man recite a hundred stanzas made up of senseless words, one word of the Law is better, which if a man hears, he becomes quiet.

103. If one man conquer in battle a thousand times a thousand men, and if another conquers himself, he is the greatest of conquerors.

104, 105. One's own self conquered is better than the conquest of all other people ; not even a god or a demigod or Māra with Brahmā can change into defeat the victory of a man who has vanquished himself.

106. If a man for a hundred years sacrifice month after month at the cost of a thousand (pieces of money), and if he but for one moment pay homage to a man whose soul is grounded (in true knowledge), better is that homage than a sacrifice for a thousand years.

107. If a man for a hundred years tend the sacrificial fire in the forest, and if he but for one moment pay homage to a man whose soul is grounded (in true knowledge), better is that homage than sacrifice for a hundred years.

108. Whatever a man sacrifices in this world as an offering

or as an oblation for a whole year in order to gain merit — (all this) is not worth the fourth part of that better offering, reverence for the upright.

109. If a man has the habit of reverence and ever respects the aged, four things will increase to him: life, beauty, happiness, power.

110. But whoso lives a hundred years, vicious and unrestrained — a life of one day is better if a man is virtuous and thoughtful.

111. And whoso lives a hundred years, foolish and uncontrolled — a life of one day is better if a man is wise and thoughtful.

112. And whoso lives a hundred years idle and weak, a life of one day is better if a man has attained firmness and strength.

113. And whoso lives a hundred years not seeing beginning and end, a life of one day is better if a man sees beginning and end.

114. And whoso lives a hundred years not seeing the immortal place, a life of one day is better if a man sees the immortal place.

115. And whoso lives a hundred years, not seeing the highest law — a life of one day is better if a man sees the highest law.

CHAPTER IX

EVIL

116. Let a man make haste to do good, let him restrain his thought from evil ; if a man does what is good slothfully, his mind delights in evil.

117. If a man commits a sin, let him not do it habitually ; let him not rejoice therein ; sorrow is the outcome of evil.

118. If a man does what is good, let him do it habitually, let him rejoice therein ; happiness is the outcome of good.

119. Even an evil-doer sees happiness as long as his evil deed has not ripened ; but when his evil deed has ripened, then does the evil-doer see evil.

120. Even a good man sees evil as long as his good deed has not ripened ; but when his good deed has ripened, then does the good man see happiness.

121. Let no man think lightly of evil, saying in his heart, It will not come nigh unto me.   Even by the falling of water-drops a water-pot is filled ; the fool becomes full of evil, even if he gather it little by little.

122. Let no man think lightly of good, saying in his heart, It will not come nigh unto me.   Even by the falling of water-drops a water-pot is filled ; the steadfast man becomes full of good, even if he gather it little by little.

123. Let a man avoid evil deeds, as a merchant who has few companions and carries much wealth, avoids a dangerous road ; as a man who loves life avoids poison.

124. He who has no wound on his hand may touch poison

with his hand ; poison does not affect one who has no wound ; nor is there evil for one who does not commit evil.

125. Whosoever offends a harmless, pure and innocent person, the evil falls back upon that fool, like light dust thrown up against the wind.

126. Some people are born again ; evil-doers go to hell ; righteous people go to heaven ; those who are free from all evil propensities attain Nirvāna.

127. Not in the sky, not in the midst of the sea, not if one enters into the clefts of the mountains, is there known a spot in the whole world, where if a man abide, he might be freed from an evil deed.

128. Not in the sky, not in the midst of the sea, not if one enters into the clefts of the mountains, is there known a spot in the whole world where if a man abide, death could not overcome him.

CHAPTER X

129. All men tremble at punishment, all men fear death ; remembering that thou art like unto them, do not strike or slay.

130. All men tremble at punishment, all men love life ; remembering that thou art like unto them, do not strike or slay.

131. He who, seeking his own happiness, injures or kills beings who long for happiness, will not find happiness after death.

132. He who, seeking his own happiness, does not injure or kill beings who also long for happiness, will find happiness after death.

133. Do not speak harshly to anybody ; those who are spoken to will answer thee in the same way.   Angry speech breeds trouble, thou wilt receive blows for blows.

134. If like a shattered gong, thou speakest not, then thou hast reached Nirvāna, contention is not found in thee.

135. As a cowherd with his staff drives his cows to pasture, so do Old Age and Death drive the life of men.

136. A fool does not know when he commits his evil deeds ; but the stupid man is consumed by his own deeds, as if burnt by fire.

137. He who inflicts punishment on those who deserve it not and offends against the innocent will soon come to one of these ten states :

138. He will have cruel suffering, infirmity or injury of the body, heavy affliction or loss of mind,

139. Or a misfortune coming from the King, or a fearful accusation, or death of kin, or loss of treasures,

140. Or lightning fire will burn his houses, and upon the dissolution of his body the fool will go to hell.

141. Not nakedness, not matted locks, not dirt, not fasting, or sleeping on the bare earth, not rubbing with dust, not sitting motionless can purify a mortal who has not overcome his doubts.

142. He who, though richly adorned, exercises tranquillity, is quiet, subdued, restrained, chaste, and has ceased to injure all other beings, is indeed a Brahman, an ascetic, a friar.

143. Is there in this world a man so restrained by modesty that he bears reproof, as a well-trained horse the whip ?

144. Like a well-trained horse when touched by the whip, be ye ardent and active ; by faith, by virtue, by energy, by meditation, by discernment of the Law, you will cast off this heavy burden of grief, perfect in knowledge and in behaviour and ever heedful.

145. Irrigators guide the water (wherever they like) ; fletchers bend the arrow ; carpenters bend a log of wood ; good people fashion themselves.

CHAPTER XI

146. How is there laughter, how is there joy, as this world is always burning ? Why do ye not seek a light, ye who are shrouded in darkness ?

147. Look at this painted image, covered with wounds, huddled together, sickly, which has no strength, no hold !

148. This body is wasted, frail, a nest of disease ; this heap of corruption breaks to pieces, life indeed ends in death.

149. Those bleaching bones, like gourds thrown away in the autumn, what pleasure is there in looking at them ?

150. After a stronghold has been made of the bones, it is covered with flesh and blood, and there dwell in it old age and death, pride and deceit.

151. The brilliant chariots of kings wear away, the body likewise waxes old, but the virtue of good people knows not age, — thus do the good say to the good.

152. A man who has learnt little, grows old like an ox ; his flesh grows but his knowledge does not grow.

153, 154. Looking for the maker of this tabernacle I ran to no avail through a round of many births ; and wearisome is birth again and again. But now, maker of the tabernacle, thou hast been seen ; thou shalt not rear this tabernacle again. All thy rafters are broken, thy ridge-pole is shattered ; the mind approaching the Eternal, has attained to the extinction of all desires.

155. Men who have not led a religious life and have not laid up treasure in their youth, perish like old herons in a lake without fish.

156. Men who have not lived a religious life, and have not laid up treasure in their youth lie like worn-out bows, sighing after the past.

CHAPTER XII

157. If a man hold himself dear, let him guard himself carefully ; during one at least of the three watches of the night a wise man should keep vigil.

158. Let each man establish himself first in the way he should go, then let him teach others ; (so doing) the wise man will have no cause to grieve.

159. If a man make himself as he teaches others to be, then being himself well subdued, he may subdue (others) ; one's own self is indeed difficult to subdue.

160. Self is the lord of self, who else could be the lord ? With self well subdued, a man finds a lord difficult to find.

161. The evil done by oneself, self-begotten, self-nursed, crushes the foolish, even as a diamond grinds a hard gem.

162. Even as a creeper over-spreads (and drags down) a Sal tree, so a man's wickedness, when it is very great, brings him to that state where his enemy wishes him to be.

163. Bad deeds and deeds harmful to ourselves are easy to do ; what is salutary and good, that is very difficult to do.

164. The foolish man who scorns the teaching of the saintly, of the noble, of the virtuous, and follows false doctrine, bears fruit to his own destruction, like the Katthaka reed.

165. By oneself the evil is done, by oneself one is defiled. Purity and impurity belong to oneself, no one can purify another.

166. Let no one forget his own good for the sake of another's, however great ; let a man, after he has discerned what this good is, be ever intent upon it.

CHAPTER XIII

THE WORLD

167. Do not follow the evil law! Do not live on in thoughtlessness! Do not follow false doctrines! Be not a friend of the world.

168, 169. Rouse thyself! Do not be idle! Follow the path of righteousness and shun transgression. The righteous man rests in bliss, in this world and in the next.

170. Look upon the world as a bubble, look upon it as a mirage : the king of death does not see him who thus looks down upon the world.

171. Come, look at this glittering world, like unto a royal chariot ; the foolish are immersed in it, but the discerning do not cling to it.

172. He who was formerly slothful and afterwards overcomes his sloth, brightens up this world, like the moon when freed from clouds.

173. He whose misdeeds are covered by good deeds, brightens up this world, like the moon when freed from clouds.

174. This world is dark, few only can see here ; a few only go to heaven, like birds escaped from the net.

175. The swans go on the path of the sun ; they go through the ether by means of their miraculous power ; the resolute rise above the world when they have conquered Māra and his train.

176. If a man has transgressed a single precept, if he speaks lies and scoffs at another world, there is no evil he will not do.

177. The niggardly do not go to the world of the gods; fools only do not praise liberality; a wise man rejoices in liberality, and through it becomes blessed in the other world.

178. Better than sovereignty over the earth, better than going to heaven, better than lordship over all worlds, is the reward of the first step in holiness.

CHAPTER XIV

BUDDHA (THE AWAKENED)

179. He whose conquest is not conquered again, into whose conquest no one in this world enters, by what track can you lead him, the Awakened, the all-perceiving, the trackless ?

180. He whom no craving with its snares and poisons can lead astray, by what track can you lead him, the Awakened, the all-perceiving, the trackless ?

181. Even the gods envy those who are awakened and mindful, who are given to meditation, who are steadfast and delight in the peace of retirement (from the world).

182. Difficult is it to obtain birth as a human being, difficult is the life of mortals, difficult is the hearing of the true Law, difficult is the rise of the Buddhas.

183. To refrain from all evil, to achieve the good, to purify one's own heart — this is the teaching of the Awakened.

184. Patience, long-suffering, is the highest form of penance, Nirvāna the highest of all things, say the Awakened ; for he is not an anchorite who strikes another, he is not an ascetic who insults another.

185. Not to blame, not to strike, to live restrained under the precepts, to be moderate in eating, to sleep and sit alone, and to dwell on lofty thoughts, — this is the teaching of the Awakened.

186. There is no satisfying lusts even by a shower of gold-pieces ; he who knows that lusts have a short taste and bring suffering in their train is wise.

187. Even in heavenly pleasures he finds no delight ; the follower of the Supremely Enlightened One (Buddha) delights only in the destruction of every craving.

188. Men driven by fear go to many a refuge, to mountains and forests, to shrines and graves and sacred trees.

189. But that is not a safe refuge, that is not the best refuge ; a man is not delivered from all pains after having gone to that refuge.

190. He who takes refuge with Buddha, the Law and the Order ; he who with clear understanding sees the four noble truths : —

191. Suffering, the origin of suffering, the destruction of suffering, and the eightfold noble path that leads to the release from suffering —

192. That is the safe refuge, that is the best refuge ; having gone to that refuge, a man is delivered from all suffering.

193. A supernatural person (a Buddha) is not easily found, he is not born everywhere. The family in which such a sage is born prospers.

194. Happy is the arising of the Awakened, happy is the teaching of the true Law, happy is harmony in the Order ; happy is the devotion of those who dwell in harmony.

195, 196. Whoso pays homage to those who deserve homage, whether the Awakened or their disciples, those who have overcome the hosts of evils and crossed the flood of sorrow, who have found deliverance and know no fear — his merit can never be measured by anyone.

CHAPTER XV

HAPPINESS

197. Let us live happily then, not hating those who hate us! Among men who hate us, let us dwell free from hatred!

198. Let us live happily then, free from ailments among the ailing! Among men who are ailing, let us dwell free from ailments!

199. Let us live happily then, free from greed among the greedy! Among men who are greedy let us dwell free from greed!

200. Let us live happily then, though we call nothing our own! We shall be like the bright gods, feeding on happiness.

201. Victory breeds hatred, for the conquered is unhappy. He who has given up both victory and defeat, he, the contented, is happy.

202. There is no fire like lust; there is no losing throw like hatred; there is no pain like this body; there is no happiness higher than peace.

203. Hunger is the greatest affliction, the body the chief source of sorrow; if one knows this truly, that is Nirvāna, the highest happiness.

204. Health is the greatest of blessings, contentedness the best riches; trust is the best of relationships, Nirvāna the highest happiness.

205. He who has tasted the sweetness of solitude and tranquillity, is free from fear and sin, while he drinks in the nectar of the Law.

206. The sight of the noble is good, to live with them is always blessedness ; if a man did not see fools, he would be truly happy.

207. He who consorts with fools suffers a long journey ; company with fools, as with an enemy, is always painful ; company with the steadfast is pleasant like meeting with kinsfolk.

208. Therefore one should follow the wise, the intelligent, the learned, the much enduring, the dutiful, the noble ; one should follow a good and wise man, as the moon follows the path of the stars.

CHAPTER XVI

PLEASURE

209. He who gives himself to vanity and does not give himself to meditation, forgetting the real aim of life and grasping at the pleasurable, will come to envy him who has exerted himself in meditation.

210. Let no man ever cleave to things that are pleasant or to those that are unpleasant. Not to see what is pleasant is pain, and it is pain to see what is unpleasant.

211. One should not therefore hold anything dear. Its loss is grievous. Those who hold nothing dear and hate nothing have no fetters.

212. From pleasure comes grief, from pleasure comes fear; he who is free from pleasure neither sorrows nor fears.

213. From (earthly) affection comes grief, from (earthly) affection comes fear; he who is free from (earthly) affection neither sorrows nor fears.

214. From (sensuous) delight comes grief, from (sensuous) delight comes fear; he who is free from (sensuous) delight neither sorrows nor fears.

215. From lust comes grief, from lust comes fear; he who is free from lust neither sorrows nor fears.

216. From craving comes grief, from craving comes fear; he who is free from craving neither sorrows nor fears.

217. He who possesses character and discrimination, who is just, speaks the truth, and does what is his own business, him the world will hold dear.

218. He in whom a desire for the Ineffable has sprung up, whose mind is permeated by this desire and whose thoughts are not bewildered by sensuality, is said to be 'bound up-stream.'

219. Kinsmen, friends, and well-wishers salute a man who has been long away, and returns safe from afar.

220. In like manner his good works receive him who has done good, and has gone from this world to the other ; — as kinsmen receive one who is dear to them on his return.

CHAPTER XVII

ANGER

221. Let a man put away anger, let him forsake pride, let him overcome all bondage! No sufferings befall the man who is not sunk in self, and who calls nothing his own.

222. He who holds back rising anger like a rolling chariot, him I call a real driver ; other people are but holding the reins.

223. Let a man overcome anger by mildness, let him overcome evil by good ; let him overcome the niggard by liberality, the liar by truth !

224. Speak the truth, do not yield to anger ; give (of thy little) if thou art asked for little ; by these three steps thou wilt attain the world of the gods.

225. The sages who do no injury, who always control their bodies, go to the unchanging place, where, having gone, they sorrow no more.

226. Those who are ever watchful, who study day and night and who strive after Nirvāna, their evil passions will come to an end.

227. There is an old saying, O Atula, — it is not only of today : 'They blame him who sits silent, they blame him who speaks much, they also blame him who says little.' There is no one in the world who is not blamed.

228. There never was, there never will be, nor is there now, a man who is always blamed, or a man who is always praised.

229, 230. But he whom those who discriminate praise
continually day after day, as without blemish, wise,
rich in knowledge and goodness — who would dare
to blame him any more than a coin made of gold
from the Jambū river ?   Even the gods praise such
a man, he is praised even by Brahmā.

231. Beware of bodily anger, and control thy body !
Leave the sins of the body, and with thy body practise virtue.

232. Beware of the anger of the tongue, and control thy
tongue !   Leave the sins of the tongue and practise
virtue with thy tongue !

233. Beware of the anger of the mind, and control thy
mind !   Leave the sins of the mind and practise virtue with thy mind.

234. The steadfast who control body, tongue, and mind
are indeed well-controlled.

CHAPTER XVIII

235. Thou art now like a sear leaf, the messengers of Death (Yama) have come near to thee ; thou standest at the threshold of thy departure, and thou hast no provision for thy journey.

236. Make thyself an island, exert thyself, and that promptly, be wise ! When thy impurities are blown away, and thou art free from guilt, thou wilt enter into the heavenly world of the elect.

237. Thy life has come to an end, thou art come near to Death (Yama), there is no resting place for thee on the road, and thou hast no provision for thy journey.

238. Make thyself an island, exert thyself and that promptly, be wise ! When thy impurities are blown away and thou art free from guilt, thou will not again enter into birth and decay.

239. Let a wise man blow away his own impurities as a smith blows away the impurities of silver, one by one, little by little, and from instant to instant.

240. As rust sprung from iron eats into its own source, so do their own deeds bring transgressors to an evil end.

241. The taint of prayers is non-repetition ; the taint of houses ill-repair ; the taint of (bodily) beauty is sloth ; the taint of a watchman, lack of vigilance.

242. Lewd conduct is the taint of woman, niggardliness the taint of a benefactor ; tainted are all evil ways in this world and the next.

243. But there is a taint worse than all taints, — ignorance is the greatest taint. O mendicants ! throw off that taint and become taintless.

244. Life is easy to live for a man who is without shame, bold after the fashion of a crow, a mischief-maker, an insulting, arrogant, and dissolute fellow.

245. But life is hard to live for a modest man, who always looks for what is pure, who is free from attachment, unassuming, spotless, and of clear vision.

246. He who destroys life, who speaks untruth, who in this world takes what is not given him, who goes to another man's wife ;

247. And the man who gives himself to drinking intoxicating liquors, he, even in this world, digs up his own root.

248. O man, know this, that the intemperate are in a bad state ; take care that greediness and vice do not bring thee to grief for a long time.

249. People give according to their faith or according to their pleasure : if a man frets about the food and the drink given to others, he will not attain tranquillity either by day or by night.

250. He in whom that feeling is destroyed and taken out by the very root, will attain tranquillity by day and by night.

251. There is no fire like lust, there is no spark like hatred, there is no snare like folly, there is no torrent like greed.

252. The fault of others is easily perceived, but that of one's self is difficult to perceive ; a man winnows his neighbours' faults like chaff, but hides his own, even as a dishonest gambler hides a losing throw.

253. If a man looks after the faults of others and is always inclined to take offence, his own evil propensities

will grow ; far indeed is such a man from their destruction.

254. There is no path through the air : no (true) monk is found outside (the Buddhist Order). The world delights in vanity, the Tathāgatas (Buddhas) are free from vanity.

255. There is no path through the air ; no (true) monk is found outside (the Buddhist Order). Nought in the phenomenal world abides, but the Awakened (the Buddhas) are never shaken.

CHAPTER XIX

THE JUST

256, 257. A man is not just if he carries a matter by violence ; no, he who distinguishes both right and wrong, who is learned and leads others, not by violence but justly and righteously, and who is guarded by the Law and intelligent, he is called just.

258. A man is not learned because he talks much ; he who is patient, free from hatred and fear, he is called learned.

259. A man is not a pillar of the Law because he talks much ; even if a man has heard but little of the Law, but sees it bodily, he is a pillar of the Law, a man who never neglects the Law.

260. A man is not an elder because his head is grey ; his age may be ripe, but he is called 'Old-in-vain.'

261. He in whom there is truth, virtue, gentleness, self-control, moderation, he who is steadfast and free from impurity, is rightly called an elder.

262. An envious, parsimonious, deceitful man does not become respectable merely by much talking or by the beauty of his complexion.

263. He in whom all this is destroyed, and taken out by the very root, he, when freed from hatred and wise, is called respectable.

264. Not by tonsure does an undisciplined man who speaks falsehood become a monk ; can a man be a monk who is still held captive by lust and greediness ?

265. He who always quiets the evil whether small or large, he is called a Samana (a quiet man) because he has quieted all evil.

266. A man is not a mendicant simply because he asks others for alms — not even if he has professed the whole Law.

267. He who is beyond merit and demerit, who lives chastely, who with knowledge passes through the world, is truly called a mendicant.

268, 269. A man is not a sage (*muni*) because he observes silence (*mona*), if he is foolish and ignorant ; but the man who, taking the balance, chooses the good and rejects the evil, is a sage and for that very reason. He who understands both worlds is therefore called a sage.

270. A man is not one of the Noble (*Ariya*) because he injures living creatures ; he is so called because he refrains from injuring all living creatures.

271, 272. Not merely by discipline and vows, nor again by much learning, not by entering into meditation, nor yet by sleeping apart do I earn the bliss of release which no worldling can know. Monk, be not confident as long as thou hast not attained the extinction of desire.

CHAPTER XX

THE WAY

273. The best of ways is the eightfold; the best of truths the four sayings; the best of states passionless; the best of men he who has eyes to see.

274. This is the way, there is no other that leads to purity of vision. Go on this way! So shall ye confound Māra (the tempter).

275. If you go on this way you will make an end of suffering. The way was taught by me when I had understood the removal of the arrow of grief.

276. You yourself must make an effort. The Tathāgatas (Buddhas) are only teachers. The meditative who enter the way are freed from the bondage of Māra.

277. 'All existing things are transient.' He who knows and sees this ceases to be the thrall of grief.

278. 'All existing things are involved in suffering.' He who knows and perceives this ceases to be the thrall of grief.

279. 'All existing things are unreal.' He who knows and perceives this is no longer the thrall of grief.

280. He who does not rouse himself when it is time to rise, who though young and strong is full of sloth, whose will and thought are weak, that lazy and idle man will never find the way to wisdom.

281. Watching his speech, well restrained in mind, let a man never commit any wrong with his body. Let a man but keep those roads of action clear, and he will achieve the way which is taught by the wise.

282. Through meditation wisdom is won, through lack of meditation wisdom is lost ; let a man who knows this double path of gain and loss so conduct himself that wisdom may grow.

283. Cut down the whole forest (of lust), not a tree only ! Danger comes out of the forest (of lust) ; when you have cut down the forest (of lust) and its undergrowth, then, monks, you will be rid of the forest and free !

284. So long as the love, even the smallest, of man towards woman is not destroyed, so long is his mind in bondage, as the calf that drinks milk is to its mother.

285. Cut out the love of self like an autumn lotus with thy hand ! Cherish the road of peace. The Happy One has shown the way to Nirvāna.

286. 'Here I shall dwell in the rain, here in winter and summer,' thus the fool fancies and does not think of his death.

287. Death comes and carries off that man absorbed in his children and flocks, his mind distracted, as a flood carries off a sleeping village.

288. Sons are no help, nor a father, nor relations ; there is no help from kinsfolk for one whom Death has seized.

289. A wise and good man who knows the meaning of this should quickly clear the way that leads to Nirvāna.

CHAPTER XXI

MISCELLANEOUS

290. If by leaving a small pleasure one sees a great pleasure, let a wise man leave the small pleasure and look to the great.

291. He who by causing pain to others wishes to obtain happiness for himself, he, entangled in the bonds of hatred, will never be free from hatred.

292. What ought to be done is neglected, what ought not to be done is done ; the evil proclivities of unruly, heedless people are always increasing.

293. But they who, ever alert, meditate on (the evils of) the body, do not follow what ought not to be done, but steadfastly do what ought to be done. The evil proclivities of watchful and wise people will come to an end.

294. A (true) Brahman goes scatheless, is free from sorrow and remorse though he have killed father and mother, and two kings of the warrior caste, though he has destroyed a kingdom with all its subjects.*

295. A (true) Brahman is free from sorrow and remorse, though he have killed father and mother, and two Brahman kings and an eminent man besides.

296. The disciples of Gotama are always wide awake and watchful, and their thoughts day and night are ever set on Buddha.

297. The disciples of Gotama are always wide awake and watchful, and their thoughts day and night are ever set on the Law.

---

* Professor W. E. Clark suggests that the Pāli word *anīgha* is almost impossible of translation. The idea this passage conveys is : 'See how happy and serene is this man who follows my religious way of life even though he has committed very great sins.'

298. The disciples of Gotama are always wide awake and watchful, and their thoughts day and night are ever set on the Order.

299. The disciples of Gotama are always wide awake and watchful, and their thoughts day and night are ever set on the body.

300. The disciples of Gotama are always wide awake and watchful, and their mind day and night ever delights in compassion.

301. The disciples of Gotama are always wide awake and thoughtful, and their mind day and night ever delights in meditation.

302. Hard is the life of a recluse — hard to enjoy. (On the other hand) the householder's life is difficult and burdensome. Painful is it to dwell with unequals. The wayfarer (again) is beset by pain ; therefore one should not be a wayfarer and one will not be beset by pain.

303. Whatever place a faithful, virtuous, celebrated and wealthy man frequents, there he is held in honour.

304. Good people shine from afar, like the peaks of Himalay ; bad people are not seen here, like arrows shot by night.

305. He who, unwearied, sits alone, sleeps alone, and walks alone, who, alone, subdues himself, will find delight in the outskirts of the forest.

CHAPTER XXII

THE DOWNWARD COURSE

306. He who says what is not, goes to hell, he also who, having done a thing, says I have not done it. After death both are equal, they are men with evil deeds in the next world.

307. Many men whose shoulders are covered with the yellow robe are of bad character and unrestrained ; such evil-doers by their evil deeds go to hell.

308. Better it would be to swallow a heated iron ball like flaring fire, than to live, a bad, unrestrained fellow, on the charity of the land.

309. Four things befall the heedless man who courts his neighbour's wife — first, acquisition of demerit, secondly, an uncomfortable bed, thirdly, evil report, and lastly, hell.

310. There is acquisition of demerit, and the downward path (to hell), there is the short pleasure of the frightened in the arms of the frightened, and the imposition by the king of heavy punishment ; therefore let no man think of his neighbour's wife.

311. As a grass-blade, if badly grasped, cuts the hand, badly-practised asceticism leads to hell.

312. An act carelessly performed, a broken vow, and a wavering obedience to religious discipline, — all this bears no great fruit.

313. If anything is to be done, let a man do it, let him attack it vigorously ! A lax ascetic only scatters the dust (of his passions) more widely.

314. An evil deed is better left undone, for a man feels remorse for it afterwards ; a good deed is better done, for having done it, one does not feel remorse.

315. Like a well-guarded frontier fort, with defences within and without, so let a man guard himself. Not a moment should escape, for they who allow the right moment to pass, suffer pain when they are in hell.

316. They who are ashamed of what they ought not to be ashamed of, and are not ashamed of what they ought to be ashamed of, such men, embracing false doctrines, enter the downward path.

317. They who fear when they ought not to fear, and fear not when they ought to fear, such men, embracing false doctrines, enter the downward path.

318. They who see sin where none exists, and do not see it where it does exist, such men, embracing false doctrines, enter the downward path.

319. They who know what is forbidden as forbidden, and what is not forbidden as not forbidden, such men, embracing the true doctrine, enter the good path.

CHAPTER XXIII

THE ELEPHANT

320. Patiently shall I endure abuse as the elephant in battle endures the arrow sent from the bow : for the world is ill-natured.

321. They lead a tamed elephant to battle, the king mounts a tamed elephant ; the tamed is the best among men, he who patiently endures abuse.

322. Mules are good if tamed, and noble Sindhu horses, and great elephants ; but he who tames himself is better still.

323. For with these riding-animals does no man reach the untrodden country to which tamed, one must go upon the tamed, namely, upon one's own well-tamed self.

324. The elephant called Dhanapālaka, his temples running with *must*,* and difficult to hold, does not eat a morsel when bound ; the elephant longs for the elephant grove.

325. If a man becomes lazy and a great eater, if he is sleepy and rolls himself round like a great hog fed on wash, that fool is born again and again.

326. This mind of mine went formerly wandering about as it liked, as it listed, as it pleased ; but I shall now control it perfectly as a rider controls with his hook a rutting elephant.

327. Delight in earnestness, guard well your thoughts. Draw yourself out of the evil way, like an elephant sunk in mud.

* See Franklin Edgerton, *The Elephant-Lore of the Hindus* (Yale University Press), pp. 29–38.

328. If a man find a prudent companion to walk with, one who is upright and steadfast, he may walk with him, overcoming all dangers, happy but considerate.

329. If a man find no prudent companion to walk with, no one who is upright and steadfast, let him walk alone like a king who has left his conquered country behind, — like an elephant in the forest.

330. It is better to live alone, there is no companionship with a fool ; let a man walk alone, let him commit no sin, (let him do) with few wishes, like an elephant in the forest.

331. If an occasion arises friends are pleasant ; enjoyment is pleasant when one shares it with another ; a good work is pleasant in the hour of death ; the giving up of all grief is pleasant.

332. Pleasant in this world is the state of a mother, pleasant the state of a father, pleasant the state of a monk, pleasant the state of a Brahman.

333. Pleasant is virtue lasting to old age, pleasant is a faith firmly rooted, pleasant is the attainment of intelligence, pleasant is avoiding of sins.

CHAPTER XXIV

THIRST

334. The thirst of a heedless man grows like a creeper ; he runs from life to life, like a monkey seeking fruit in the forest.

335. Whomsoever, haunted by this fierce thirst, the world overcomes, his sufferings increase like the abounding bīrana grass.

336. But whoso overcomes this fierce thirst difficult to conquer in this world, sufferings fall from him like water-drops from a lotus leaf.

337. Therefore this with your kind leave I say unto you, to all who are here assembled : Dig up the root of thirst, as he who wants the sweet-scented usīra root must dig up the bīrana grass, lest Māra crush you again and again, even as a stream crushes the reeds.

338. As a tree though it be cut down grows up again as long as its root is sound and firm, even thus if the proneness to thirst be not destroyed, this pain (of life) will return again and again.

339. The misguided man whose thirst, running towards pleasure, is exceeding strong in the thirty-six channels, the waves will sweep away — namely his desires that incline to lust.

340. The currents run in all directions, the creeper (of passion) stands sprouting ; if you see the creeper springing up, cut its root by means of wisdom.

341. A creature's pleasures are extravagant and luxurious ; sunk in lust and looking for happiness men undergo (again and again) birth and decay.

342. Men driven on by thirst run about like a hunted hare ; held in fetters and bonds they undergo pain for a long time again and again.

343. Men driven on by thirst run about like a hunted hare ; let therefore the mendicant who desires to be free from lust, banish thirst.

344. He who, free from desire, gives himself up to desire again ; who, having escaped from this jungle, runs back into it — come behold that man, though released he runs back into bondage.

345. Wise people do not call that a strong fetter which is made of iron or wood or hemp ; far stronger is the passionate devotion to precious stones and rings, to sons and wives.

346. That bond wise people call strong which drags down, and, though yielding, is hard to undo ; having cut this (bond) people retire from the world with no backward glance, leaving behind the pleasures of sense.

347. Those who are immersed in lust, run down the stream (of desires) as a spider runs down the web which he himself has spun ; having cut this (bond), the steadfast retire from the world, with no backward glance, leaving all sorrow behind.

348. Give up what is before, give up what is behind, give up what is in the middle ; cross to the Further Shore (of existence) ; if thy mind is altogether free, thou wilt not again enter into birth and decay.

349. If a man is tossed about by doubts, swayed by strong passions and yearning only for what is delightful, his thirst will grow more and more and he will indeed make his fetters strong.

350. If a man delights in quieting doubts and, ever-mindful, meditates on what is not pleasant, he cer-

tainly will remove, nay, he will cut the fetter of Māra.

351. He that has reached perfection, he that does not tremble, he that is without thirst and without sin, has broken all the thorns of life : this will be his last body.

352. He who is without thirst and without attachment, who understands the words of the ancient dialect, who knows the order of letters — those which are before and which are after — is truly wise ; he has received his last body.

353. I have conquered all, I know all ; in all conditions of life I am free from taint ; I have left all, and through the destruction of thirst I am free ; having by myself attained supernatural knowledge, to whom can I point as my teacher ?

354. The gift of the Law exceeds all gifts ; the sweetness of the Law exceeds all sweetness, the delight in the Law exceeds all delights ; the extinction of thirst overcomes all suffering.

355. Riches destroy the foolish, if they look not for the other shore ; by his thirst for riches the foolish man destroys himself as if he were his own enemy.

356. The fields are damaged by weeds, mankind is damaged by lust : therefore a gift bestowed on those who are free from lust brings great reward.

357. The fields are damaged by weeds, mankind is damaged by hatred : therefore a gift bestowed on those who do not hate brings great reward.

358. The fields are damaged by weeds, mankind is damaged by delusion : therefore a gift bestowed on those who are free from delusion brings great reward.

359. The fields are damaged by weeds, mankind is damaged by craving : therefore a gift bestowed on those who are free from craving, brings great reward.

CHAPTER XXV

360. Restraint in the eye is good, good is restraint in the ear, in the nose restraint is good, good is restraint in the tongue.

361. In the body restraint is good, good is restraint in speech, in thought restraint is good, good is restraint in all things. A monk restrained in all things, is freed from all suffering.

362. He who controls his hand, he who controls his feet, he who controls his speech, he who is well controlled, he who delights inwardly, who is collected, who is solitary and content, he is truly called a monk.

363. The monk who controls his tongue, who speaks wisely, who is not puffed up, who elucidates the letter and the spirit of the Law, his word is sweet.

364. The monk who has made of the Law his garden of delight, pondering and recollecting it, will never fall away from the good Law.

365. Let him not disdain what he has received, let him not envy others; a monk who envies others does not attain (the tranquillity of) meditation.

366. A monk who, though he has received little, does not disdain what he has received, even the gods will praise as of pure life and free from indolence.

367. He who never identifies himself with name and form, and does not grieve over what is not, is indeed called a monk.

368. The monk who abides in loving-kindness, who is

calm in the doctrine of Buddha, will reach the quiet place, emancipation from the transitory, and happiness.

369. O monk, bale out this boat! If emptied it will go quickly; having cut off lust and hatred, thou wilt reach Nirvāna.

370. Cut off five, renounce five, cultivate five more. A monk who has escaped from the five fetters is called 'One who has crossed the flood.'

371. Meditate, O monk, and be not heedless! Set not thy heart on the pleasures of sense that thou mayest not for thy heedlessness have to swallow the iron ball (in hell), and that thou mayest not cry out in the midst of fire, 'This is pain.'

372. Without knowledge there is no meditation, without meditation there is no knowledge: he who has both knowledge and meditation is near unto Nirvāna.

373. A monk who with tranquil mind has entered his empty house feels a more than earthly delight when he gains a clear perception of the Law.

374. As soon as he has grasped the origin and passing away of the elements of the body, he attains the happiness and joy which belong to those who know the immortal.

375. And this is the beginning here for a wise monk: watchfulness over the senses, contentedness, restraint under the precepts; let him keep noble friends whose lives are pure and who are not slothful;

376. Let him live in charity, let him be perfect in his behaviour; then in fullness of delight he will make an end of suffering.

377. As the jasmine sheds its withered flowers, even so, O monks, men should shed lust and hatred.

378. The monk who is quiet in body, speech, and mind,

who is collected and has refused the baits of the world, is truly called tranquil.

379. Rouse thyself by thyself, examine thyself by thyself ; thus self-guarded and mindful, wilt thou, O monk, live happily.

380. For self is the lord of self, self is the refuge of self, therefore curb thyself as the merchant curbs a good horse.

381. The monk, full of delight, who is firm in the doctrine of Buddha will reach the quiet place, cessation of the mortal and transitory, and happiness.

382. The young monk who applies himself to Buddha's teaching, lights up this world like the moon freed from clouds.

CHAPTER XXVI

383. Cut off the stream valiantly, drive away the desires, O Brahman ! When you have understood the dissolution of all that is made you will understand that which is not made.

384. When the Brahman has reached the other shore in two states (tranquillity and insight), he is freed from all bonds as a result of his knowledge.

385. The man for whom there is neither this nor that shore, nor both — him, the fearless and unshackled, I call indeed a Brahman.

386. Whoso is meditative, blameless, settled, dutiful, without passions, and who has attained the highest end, him I call indeed a Brahman.

387. The sun is bright by day, the moon shines by night, the Brahman is bright in his meditation ; but Buddha, the Awakened, is bright with splendour day and night.

388. Because a man has put away evil, therefore he is called a Brahman ; because he walks quietly, therefore he is called a Samana (ascetic) ; because he has banished his own impurities, therefore he is called a Pabbajita (religious recluse).

389. No one should attack a Brahman, but no Brahman (if attacked) should let himself fly at his aggressor ! Woe to him who strikes a Brahman, more woe to him who flies at his aggressor.

390. It advantages a Brahman not a little if he holds his

mind back from the allurements of life; in direct measure as the wish to injure declines, suffering is quieted.

391. Him I call indeed a Brahman who does not offend by body, word or thought, and is controlled in these three respects.

392. The man from whom one has learned the Law as taught by the supremely enlightened Buddha, one should reverence profoundly, even as the Brahman worships the sacrificial fire.

393. A man does not become a Brahman by his matted locks or his lineage or his birth; in whom there is truth and righteousness, he is blessed, he is a Brahman.

394. What is the use of thy matted locks, O fool! Of what avail thy (raiment of) antelope skin? Within thee there is ravening, but the outside thou makest clean.

395. The man who wears cast-off rags, who is emaciated and covered with veins, who meditates alone in the forest, him I call indeed a Brahman.

396. I do not call a man a Brahman because of his birth or of his mother. He is supercilious in his mode of address and he is wealthy: but the poor man who is free from attachments, him I call indeed a Brahman.

397. Him I call indeed a Brahman who has cut all fetters, who never trembles, and is unshackled and emancipated.

398. He that has cut the strap, the thong, the rope and all thereto pertaining, he that has raised the bar, he that is awakened, him I call indeed a Brahman.

399. Him I call indeed a Brahman who, though innocent of all offence, endures reproach, stripes and bonds,

who has patience for his force and strength (of mind) for his army.

400. Him I call indeed a Brahman who is free from anger, dutiful, virtuous, without concupiscence, who is subdued, and has received his last body.

401. Him I call indeed a Brahman who does not cling to the pleasures of sense any more than water to a lotus leaf, or than a mustard seed to the point of a needle.

402. Him I call indeed a Brahman who even here knows the end of his suffering, has put down his burden and is unshackled.

403. Him I call indeed a Brahman whose knowledge is deep, who possesses wisdom, who knows the right way and the wrong, and has attained the highest end.

404. Him I call indeed a Brahman who keeps aloof from both householders and the houseless, who wanders about without a home and has but few desires.

405. Him I call indeed a Brahman who withholds the rod of punishment from other creatures, whether feeble or strong, and does not kill nor cause slaughter.

406. Him I call indeed a Brahman who is tolerant with the intolerant, mild among the violent, and free from greed among the greedy.

407. Him I call indeed a Brahman from whom lust and hatred, pride and envy, have dropt like a mustard seed from the point of a needle.

408. Him I call indeed a Brahman who utters true speech, instructive and free from harshness, so that he offend no one.

409. Him I call indeed a Brahman who takes nothing in the world that is not given him, be it long or short, small or large, good or bad.

410. Him I call indeed a Brahman who fosters no desires

for this world or for the next, has no inclinations and is unshackled.

411. Him I call indeed a Brahman who has no longings, who as the result of knowledge, is free from doubt and has immersed himself in the Immortal.

412. Him I call indeed a Brahman who is in this world above the bondage of both merit and demerit, who is free from grief, blameless and pure.

413. Him I call indeed a Brahman who is bright like the moon, limpid, serene, and clear, and in whom all giddiness is extinct.

414. Him I call indeed a Brahman who has traversed this miry road, difficult to pass, this world of birth and rebirth and its vanity, who has gone through and reached the other shore, who is meditative, free from lust and doubt, free from attachment, and content.

415. Him I call indeed a Brahman who, having forsaken and utterly eradicated lusts, has gone forth into the houseless state.

416. Him I call indeed a Brahman, who, having forsaken and utterly eradicated craving, has gone forth into the houseless state.

417. Him I call indeed a Brahman who, after casting off bondage to men, has risen above bondage to the gods, and is free from all and every bondage.

418. Him I call indeed a Brahman who has left what gives pleasure and what gives pain, who is cold and free from all germs (of renewed life), the hero who has conquered all the worlds.

419. Him I call indeed a Brahman who knows the passing away and rebirth of beings everywhere, who is free from attachment, happy and awakened.

420. Him I call indeed a Brahman, whose future estate the gods do not know, nor spirits, nor men, whose

evil proclivities are extinct and who has become a saint (Arhat).

421. Him I call indeed a Brahman who calls nothing his own, whether it pertains to past, present, or future, who is poor and free from grasping.

422. Him I call indeed a Brahman, — the manly, the noble, the hero, the great seer, the conqueror, the impassible, the sinless, the awakened.

423. Him I call indeed a Brahman who knows his former abodes, who sees heaven and hell and has reached the end of births, a sage who has attained the fullness of knowledge, and all of whose perfections are perfect.

BUDDHA AND THE OCCIDENT

THE special danger of the present time would seem to be an increasing material contact between national and racial groups that remain spiritually alien. The chief obstacle to a better understanding between East and West in particular is a certain type of Occidental who is wont to assume almost unconsciously that the East has everything to learn from the West and little or nothing to give in return. One may distinguish three main forms of this assumption of superiority on the part of the Occidental : first, the assumption of racial superiority, an almost mystical faith in the preëminent virtues of the white peoples (especially Nordic blonds) as compared with the brown or yellow races ; secondly, the assumption of superiority based on the achievements of physical science and the type of 'progress' it has promoted, a tendency to regard as a general inferiority the inferiority of the Oriental in material efficiency ; thirdly, the assumption of religious superiority, less marked now than formerly, the tendency to dismiss non-Christian Asiatics *en masse* as 'heathen,' or else to recognize value in their religious beliefs, notably in Buddhism, only in so far as they conform to the pattern set by Christianity. Asiatics for their part are ready enough to turn to account the discoveries of Western science, but they are even less disposed than they were before the Great War to admit the moral superiority of the West. A certain revulsion of feeling seems to be taking place even in Japan which has gone farther than any other Oriental land in its borrowings from the Occident.

On any comprehensive survey, indeed, Asiatics, so far

from having a mean estimate of themselves, have had their own conceit of superiority, not only with reference to Occidentals but with reference to one another. Many Hindus have held in the past, some no doubt still hold, that true spirituality has never appeared in the world save on the sacred soil of India. No country, again, not even ancient Greece, has been more firmly convinced than China that it alone was civilized. A statesman of the Tang period addressed to the throne a memorial against Buddhism which begins as follows : 'This Buddha was a barbarian.' One of the traditional names of China 'All-under-Heaven' (*Poo-Tien-shia*) is itself sufficiently eloquent.

In general Asia offers cultural groups so widely divergent that one may ask if there is not something artificial in any attempt to contrast an Asiatic with a European or Western point of view. A symposium * on this topic was recently held in Paris to which about one hundred and fifty French and foreign writers and scholars contributed. According to one of these contributors, M. Sylvain Lévi of the *Collège de France*, it is absurd to bring together under one label 'a Syrian of Beyrut, an Iranian of Persia, a Brahman of Benares, a pariah of the Deccan, a merchant of Canton, a mandarin of Peking, a lama of Thibet, a yacut of Siberia, a daimio of Japan, a cannibal of Sumatra, etc.' When stated in such general terms the question of East versus West has, as a matter of fact, little or no meaning. It may, however, turn out to have a very weighty meaning if properly defined and limited. Other contributors to the Paris symposium, though they express a singular variety of opinions about Asia, occasionally show some inkling of what this meaning is. They are helped to their

* *Les Appels de l'Orient:* Les Cahiers du Mois. Emile-Paul, Frères, Éditeurs. Paris.

sense of the contrast between Europe and Asia by another continental contrast — that between Europe and America ; and here they are in substantial agreement. America stands for the purely industrial and utilitarian view of life, the cult of power and machinery and material comfort. It is in order to escape from this baleful excess of Americanism that Europe is inclined to turn towards the East. 'Europe,' we read in the symposium, 'is, as a result of her almost mortal sufferings of recent years, ready to bow her head and humble herself. It will then be possible for Oriental influences to make themselves felt. An immense continent will remain the refuge and the fortress of the Occidental spirit : the whole of America will harden herself and proudly close her mind, whereas Europe will heed the lesson of the Orient.' * One may perhaps sum up the sense of passages of this kind by saying that in its pursuit of the truths of the natural order Europe had come to neglect the truths of humility — the truths of the inner life. In the literal sense of the word, it has lost its orientation, for it originally received these truths from the Orient. One remembers Arnold's account of this former contact between East and West : first, the impact of a Europe drunk with power upon Asia.

> The East bowed low before the blast
> In patient deep disdain ;
> She let the legions thunder past,
> And plunged in thought again.

And finally the heeding of the voice of the East, in other words the acceptance of the truths of the inner life in their Christian form, by a Europe that had grown weary of her own materialism :

> She heard it, the victorious West,
> In sword and crown arrayed,

* *Les Appels de l'Orient*, p. 67.

She felt the void that mined her breast,
She shivered and obeyed.

The problems that arise today in connexion with the relations of East and West are far more complex than they were in Graeco-Roman times.   The East now means not merely the Near East, but even more the Far East.   Moreover, the East, both Near and Far, is showing itself less inclined than formerly to bow before the imperialistic aggression of the Occident 'in patient deep disdain.'   On the contrary, a type of nationalistic self-assertion is beginning to appear in various Oriental lands that is only too familiar to us in the West.   Japan in particular has been disposing of her Buddhas as curios and turning her attention to battleships.   The lust of domination which is almost the ultimate fact of human nature, has been so armed in the Occident with the machinery of scientific efficiency that the Orient seems to have no alternative save to become efficient in the same way or be reduced to economic and political vassalage.   This alternative has been pressing with special acuteness on China, the pivotal country of the Far East.   Under the impact of the West an ethos that has endured for thousands of years has been crumbling amid a growing spiritual bewilderment.   In short the Orient itself is losing its orientation.   The essence of this orientation may be taken to be the affirmation in some form or other of the truths of the inner life.   Unfortunately affirmations of this kind have come to seem in the Occident a mere matter of dogma and tradition in contrast with a point of view that is positive and experimental. It is here that the study of great eastern teachers, notably Confucius and Buddha, may prove helpful.   The comparative absence of dogma in the humanism of Confucius and the religion of Buddha can scarcely be regarded as an inferiority.   On the contrary one can at least see the point of view of a young Chinese scholar, Mr. H. H. Chang, who complains that the man of the Occident has introduced unnecessary theological and metaphysical complications into religion : he has been too prone to indulge in 'weird dogmas' and 'uncanny curiosity.' He has been guilty to a degree unknown in the Far East of intolerance, obscurantism, and casuistry. Pascal, one of the most profound of religious thinkers, attacked casuistry in its Jesuitical form but himself supplies an example of what Mr. Chang means by weird dogmas. Man, says Pascal in substance, is unintelligible to himself without the belief in infant damnation.

The Far Eastern doctrine that is probably freest from the undesirable elements that Mr. Chang enumerates is the authentic teaching of Buddha. Scholarly investigation has already proceeded to a point where it is possible to speak with some confidence not only of this teaching but of Buddha himself.* One may affirm indeed that few doctrines and personalities of the remote past stand out more clearly. There is practical agreement among scholars that the material found in the Pāli Canon, the basis of the form of the religion known as the Hīnayāna or Small Vehicle, which prevails in Ceylon, Burma, and other countries, is on the whole more trustworthy than the records of the Mahāyāna or Great Vehicle, which, variously modified, prevails in Thibet, China, Korea, and Japan. The psychological evidence on this point, which is overwhelming, is supplemented by historical evidence — for example, the Asokan inscriptions. By psychological evidence I mean evidence of the same kind as is supplied by numerous passages of the New Testament, passages

---

* Numerous and intricate historical problems arise, however, in connexion with the Pāli Canon and the degree to which it may lay claim to authenticity.

that give one the immediate sense of being in the presence of a great religious teacher. Anyone who can read the Sermon on the Mount and then proceed to speculate on the 'historicity' of Jesus must simply be dismissed as incompetent in matters religious.

On the basis then of evidence both psychological and historical one must conclude that if the Far East has been comparatively free from casuistry, obscurantism, and intolerance, the credit is due in no small measure to Buddha. It is so difficult to have a deep conviction and at the same time to be tolerant that many have deemed the feat impossible. Yet not only Buddha himself but many of his followers achieved it. For example, the tolerant spirit displayed by the Emperor Asoka who probably did more than any other person to make Buddhism a world religion, simply reflects the spirit of the Founder. An apologue of Buddha's which has been widely popular in both East and West, is relevant to this topic of tolerance. Once upon a time, Buddha relates, a certain king of Benares, being bored and desiring to divert himself, gathered together a number of beggars blind from birth, and offered a prize to the beggar who should give him the best account of an elephant. The first beggar who examined the elephant chanced to lay hold upon the leg, and reported that an elephant was like a tree-trunk ; a second, laying hold of the tail, declared that an elephant was like a rope ; a third, who seized an ear, insisted that an elephant was like a palm leaf ; and so on. Whereupon the beggars proceeded to dispute with one another and finally fell to fisticuffs and the king was highly diverted. Even so, says Buddha, ordinary teachers, who have grasped this or that small member of the truth, quarrel with one another. Only a Buddha can apprehend the whole. The thought that in matters spiritual we are at best blind beggars fighting with one another in our native murk is not conducive to a narrow and fanatical intensity.   The rounded vision is so difficult, so alien, one is tempted to say, to human nature, that one is not surprised to learn that Buddhas are rare, only five at the most in a kalpa or cosmic cycle, a period, according to Hindu computation, of something over four billion years.

The apologue I have just cited suggests that Buddha was more prone to humour than most religious teachers.   The contrast in this respect between certain portions of the Pāli Canon (notably the Jātaka tales) and the Christian Bible is striking.   Another trait possessed by Buddha that is in itself humanistic rather than religious is urbanity.   The doctrine of the mean that Buddha proclaimed even in the religious life is not unrelated to the absence in Buddhism of the casuistical and obscurantist element.   There is a sense, one should remember, in which casuistry is legitimate and indeed inevitable.   The general principle needs to be adjusted to the infinitely varying circumstances of actual life.   There is casuistry in this sense in the first main division of the Pāli Canon (*Vinaya*) — the division which deals with the details of discipline in the Order (*Sangha*) founded by Buddha.   The danger here is that a minute outer regulation should encroach unduly on the moral autonomy of the individual.   Buddha, as we shall presently see more fully, was at special pains to assert this autonomy.   A second peril of casuistry is that it should not only substitute outer authority for individual conscience, but that it should be made a cover for the kind of relaxation that Pascal attacks in the *Provincial Letters*. Buddha would have the members of his Order avoid this relaxation without falling into the opposite extreme of asceticism and mortification of the flesh.   This is in substance his doctrine of the middle path.

The obscurantism that denies unduly the senses has usually been associated in the Occident with the obscurantism that denies unduly the intellect. Buddha's avoidance of this latter form of obscurantism is a matter of even more interest than his avoidance of the ascetic extreme. The conflict between the head and the heart, the tendency to repudiate the intellect either in the name of what is above or what is below it, which has played such an enormous rôle in the Occident from some of the early Christians to Bergson, is alien to genuine Buddhism. The supreme illumination of Buddha was associated with the precise tracing of cause and effect, with the following out of the so-called causal nexus. His discriminating temper appears in the care with which he uses general terms, always a crucial point in any doctrine. He gives one the impression of a person who has worked out his ideas to the ultimate degree of clarity, a clarity that is found not merely in separate propositions but in the way in which they are woven into an orderly whole. During his youth, we are told, he passed through a period of groping and hesitation, but after his illumination he never seems to grope or hesitate. This firm intellectual grasp, joined to a dominant and unwavering purpose, no doubt contributed to the effect of authority that he produced upon his contemporaries and continues to produce upon us. In his personality he strikes the reader of the old records as massive, some might say even a bit ponderous, and at the same time supremely self-reliant and aggressively masculine. One has the sense of getting very close to Buddha himself in the verses of the Sutta-Nipāta descriptive of the true sage. A few lines of this passage, which I render literally, are as follows:

> The wise man who fares strenuously apart,
> Who is unshaken in the midst of praise or blame,

Even as a lion that trembles not at noises,
Or as the wind that is not caught in a net,
Or as the lotus that is unstained by the water —
A leader of others and not by others led,
Him verily the discerning proclaim to be a sage.

In human nature, as it is actually constituted, every virtue has its cognate fault. The unflinching analysis practised by the early Buddhists runs very easily, especially when divorced from intuition, in some sense or other of that much abused word, into scholastic dryness. There are portions of the Buddhist writings that remind one in this respect of the less attractive side of the Aristotelian tradition in the West. The Buddhist again inclines at times, like the Aristotelian, to be unduly categorical and so to achieve a sort of false finality. The Buddhist commentators, for example, give what they conceive to be a definitive enumeration of the different noises that characterize a normal town ! Furthermore, large portions of the Buddhist books seem to the Western reader to have damnable iteration, to push beyond permissible grounds the sound maxim that repetition is the mother of memory. It is well to remember that most of this repetition is only a mnemonic device that would never have been employed if the canonical material had from the outset been committed to writing. And then, too, in the midst of tracts of wearisome repetition and arid categorizing one encounters not infrequently passages that are vividly metaphorical and concrete and lead one to infer in Buddha a rare gift for aphoristic utterance ; though even these passages, if one may be allowed to speak of such matters from a profane literary point of view, can scarcely match in sheer epigrammatic effectiveness certain sayings of Christ.

If the doctrine and personality of Buddha stand out so distinctly from the ancient records, how, it may be asked,

has there been so much misapprehension regarding both ?
Certain reasons for this misapprehension are obvious ; it
may be well to clear these away before coming to other
reasons which lie less near the surface. In the first place,
much confusion has been caused in the Occident by the
failure to distinguish between Mahāyāna and Hīnayāna.
Various eminent thinkers and writers of the nineteenth
century got their chief impression of Buddhism from the
extravagant theosophy of the *Lotus of the Good Law* as
translated by Eugène Burnouf. Even those who, without
knowing Pāli, have gone to the more authentic documents
have been frequently misled by the translations. The
special pitfall here is the general terms. Though these
terms, as I have said, are used by Buddha himself with considerable precision, they have no exact Occidental equiva-
lents. Translators seem at times to have given up in des-
pair the task of rendering all the discriminations of a
subtle and unfamiliar psychology. Thus it is estimated
that Fausböll, to whom we are deeply indebted for the first
edition of the Dhammapada in the West, has in his version
of the Sutta-Nipāta translated fifteen different Pāli words
by the one English word 'desire.'

Moreover, to come to less obvious sources of misapprehension, serious study of the Far East got under way during a period that was in its predominant temper either
romantic, or again, scientific and rationalistic. Neither the
romanticist nor the pure rationalist is qualified to grasp
what is specifically Oriental in the Orient. The romanticist seeks in the East what he seeks everywhere, the element of strangeness and wonder. His interest is in differences rather than in identities ; as a consequence, this
form of Orientalism has amounted chiefly in practice to
the pursuit of picturesqueness and local colour. Closely
allied to this pursuit is the quest of some place of refuge

from an unpalatable here and now.   A familiar example
is 'The Road to Mandalay,' which tells of the satisfaction
that the British private finds in Buddhist Burma of his
craving for a 'neater sweeter maiden in a cleaner greener
land.'   I may be accused of taking too seriously Kipling's
trifle, but after all this romantic imperialist has enjoyed a
certain prestige as an interpreter, not only of the Anglo-
Indian East, but of the real East.   The central passage of
'The Road to Mandalay' may therefore serve as well as
any other to illustrate the Oriental aspect of the immense
literature of escape that has grown up in connexion with
the romantic movement.

Ship me somewheres East of Suez, where the best is like the worst,
Where there ain't no Ten Commandments, an' a man may raise a
    thirst ;
For the temple bells are callin' an' it's there that I would be, —
By the old Moulmain Pagoda lookin' lazy at the sea.

If the temple bells are calling the British private to 'raise
a thirst,' to what, one may inquire, are they calling the
native Burman ?   Certainly not to be 'lazy' and irresponsi-
ble.   Kipling himself would no doubt warn us against
pursuing any such unprofitable inquiry, in virtue of the
principle that 'East is East and West is West, and never
the twain shall meet.'   The fact is that they are meeting
more and more, with the attendant danger that this meeting will be only on the material level.   Kipling's line is
rightfully resented by Orientals : it is true about in the
sense that John is John and James is James and never the
twain shall meet, or, if there is any difference between the
two statements, it is one of degree and not of kind.

If we refuse then to admit that the point of view of
Buddhist Burma is necessarily unintelligible to us and turn
for information to an authentic document like the Dhammapada, what we find is that a central admonition of

Buddha may be summed up in the phrase : Do not raise a thirst ! Nothing perhaps throws more light on what actually goes on in Burma today than the type of education given to the children of the country by the members of the Buddhist Order. This education consists largely in the memorizing of certain sacred texts. One of the passages especially favoured for this purpose, we learn from a recent book on Burma, is Buddha's discussion of the nature of true blessedness, which runs in part as follows :

To wait on mother and father, to cherish child and wife and follow a quiet calling, this is true blessedness.

To give alms, to live religiously, to protect relatives, to perform blameless deeds, this is true blessedness.

To cease from sin, to refrain from intoxicating drinks, to persevere in right conduct, this is true blessedness.

Reverence and humility, contentment and gratitude, the hearing of the Law of righteousness at fitting moments, this is true blessedness.

Patience and pleasant speech, intercourse with holy men, religious conversation at due seasons, this is true blessedness.

Penance and chastity, discernment of the noble truths and the realization of peace, this is true blessedness.

The author of the book on Burma proffers the further information that, as a result of memorizing such verses, the children acquire 'boundless charity and rigid self-control' — a statement one is inclined to receive with some scepticism. Like Kipling, though in an entirely different way, he is probably substituting an idyllic for the real Burma. But if only a fraction of what he says is true, we should seek to divert the attention of our own children from radio sets and motion-pictures and set them to memorizing Buddhist verses !

Though particular utterances of Buddha, like the discourse on True Blessedness I have just quoted, may offer little difficulty, it must be admitted that his teaching is not easy for the Westerner to grasp in its total spirit. Even the person who affirms an underlying unity in human nature and is more interested in this unity than in its picturesque modifications in time and space, should at least be able to see the point of view of the scholar who affirmed that he had turned to the study of Buddhism in order that he might enjoy 'the strangeness of the intellectual landscape.' A chief reason for this strangeness is that the doctrine of Buddha cuts across certain oppositions that have been established in Western thought since the Greeks, and have come to seem almost inevitable. There has, for example, from the time of Heraclitus and Parmenides been an opposition between the partisans of the One and the partisans of the Many, between those who see in life only change and relativity and those who in some form or other affirm an abiding unity. The Platonic affirmation in particular of a world of ideas that transcends the flux so combined with Christianity that it has come to be almost inseparable from our notion of religion. Religion, as we understand it, seems to require faith in a spiritual essence or soul that is sharply set apart from the transitory, and in a God who is conceived as the supreme 'idea' or entity. Buddha denies the soul in the Platonic sense and does not grant any place in his discipline to the idea of God. Superficially he seems to be on the side of all the 'flowing' philosophers from Heraclitus to Bergson. The schoolmen of the Middle Ages would have accounted him an uncompromising nominalist. We are told that, at the voice of a Buddha proclaiming the law of mutability in both Heaven and earth, the bright gods who had deemed themselves immortal feel a shiver of apprehension like that occasioned by the roar of the lion in the other beasts of the field. Buddha is so disconcerting to us because doctrinally he recalls the most extreme of our Occidental philosophers of the flux, and at the same time, by the type of life at which he aims, reminds us rather of the Platonist and the Christian.

Buddha also differs from the religious teachers with whom we are familiar by his positive temper. The idea of experiment and the idea of the supernatural have come to seem to us mutually exclusive. Yet Buddha may perhaps be best defined as a critical and experimental supernaturalist. If he deserves to be thus defined it is not because of the so-called magic powers (*iddhi*) — the power of supernormal memory, of levitation and the like. If we accepted only a small part of what we read in the ancient records about the thaumaturgical accomplishments not merely of Buddha but of a number of his followers, we should have to conclude that man has certain psychic capacities that have become atrophied through long disuse. In general, however, the ancient Buddhist maintained an extreme reserve in regard to the magic powers. He granted them at most a very subordinate rôle in religion. He is far removed in this respect from a Pascal who avowed, like St. Augustine before him, that he would not have accepted Christianity had it not been for its miracles.

One is justified in asserting on other than thaumaturgical grounds that the genuine teaching of Buddha is steeped in the supernatural. According to the tradition, when Buddha begged his way through the streets of his native town, his father, King Suddhodana, demurred ; whereupon Buddha said that he was merely following the practice of all his race. When the King protested that no one of his race had ever been a mendicant, Buddha replied that he referred, not to his earthly lineage, but to the race of the Buddhas. As a matter of fact, what is specifically supernatural, not merely in the Buddhas but in other re-

ligious teachers, for example in St. Francis, is their achieve-
ment of certain virtues.   Of these the virtue that marks
most immediately the obeisance of the spirit to what transcends nature and has therefore always been held, by those
who believe in such virtues at all, to command the others,
is humility.   In the present naturalistic era the very word
humility has tended to fall into disuse or, if used at all, to
be used incorrectly.   One needs to be reminded, for example, that humility and modesty are not at all synony-
mous.   Matthew Arnold says that Emerson was one of
the most modest of men, Mr. Brownell that he was one of
the least humble.   Both statements are conceivably correct.   Of Buddha, one is tempted to say that he was humble without being modest.   It is not easy to ascribe
modesty to a teacher who made claims for himself even
more sweeping than those put forth by the Founder of
Christianity.   Regarding these claims one is reminded of
an anecdote that may also serve to illustrate the peculiar
vein of humour in the Buddhist writings.   A certain Buddhist recluse, we are told, being puzzled by a knotty point
of doctrine and finding no mortal who could solve his
difficulty, at last by appropriate meditations mounted from
heaven to heaven but was still unable to discover anyone
who could enlighten him.   Finally he came to the paradise of Brahmā, and propounded the question to the di-
vinity himself.   Brahmā said, 'I am Brahmā, the Supreme
Being, the Omniscient, the Unsurpassed,' etc. 'I did not ask
you,' replied the recluse, 'whether you were Brahmā, the
Supreme Being, the Omniscient and Unsurpassed, but
whether you could answer my question.' *   Whereupon
Brahmā took him to one side and explained that the angels
of his retinue thought him omniscient, but that in fact no
one could give the desired enlightenment save Buddha.

* Kevaddha-Sutta of the Dīgha-Nikāya.

That Buddha should put himself above all other animate beings, whether men or gods, and at the same time be humble is, from the Christian point of view, highly paradoxical. The essence of humility in Christianity is the submission not merely of man's will but of the will of Christ himself to the will of a divine personality. If one is to understand how Buddha avoids asserting any such personality and at the same time retains humility one needs to reflect on what it means to be a critical and experimental supernaturalist. It means first of all that one must deny oneself the luxury of certain affirmations about ultimate things and start from the immediate data of consciousness. It is hard to see, for example, how one can affirm, on strictly experimental grounds, a personal God and personal immortality. If a man feels that these tremendous affirmations are necessary for his spiritual comfort, he should turn to dogmatic and revealed religion which alone can give them, adding with Dr. Johnson that 'the good and evil of Eternity are too ponderous for the wings of wit.' The person who assumes a genuinely critical attitude is finally forced to accept in some form or other the maxim that man is the measure of all things. If one is told in the words of Plato that not man but God is the measure of all things, the obvious reply is that man nowhere perhaps gives his own measure so clearly as in his conceptions of God ; and that is why, as Goethe would add, God is so often made a jest. What one is able to affirm without going beyond immediate experience and falling into dogma is, in Arnold's phrase, a great power not ourselves that makes for righteousness, a phrase that reminds one of Buddha's conception of the *dhamma*, or human law, as one may render it, in contradiction to the law of physical nature. Not being able to find any personality human or divine superior to his own, Buddha got his humility, as he himself tells us, by looking up to the Law.

Let us consider more carefully what this obeisance to the *dhamma* means when disengaged, as Buddha seeks to disengage it, from dogma and metaphysical assumption and envisaged as one of the immediate data of consciousness. Numerous Western philosophers from Descartes down have professed to start from these data. On comparing the results they have reached with the results reached by Buddha one is conscious of some central clash. At the risk of being unduly schematic, one may say that the tendency of Western philosophers has been to regard as primary in consciousness either thought (*cogito ergo sum*) or feeling (*sentio ergo sum*). Buddha, for his part, is neither a rationalist nor, again, an emotionalist. No small confusion has resulted from trying to fit him into one or the other of these alien categories. He gives the primary place to will, but to a quality of will that has been almost inextricably bound up in the Occident with the doctrine of divine grace and has been obscured in direct proportion to the decline of this doctrine. The question of the priority of will in this sense, as compared either with intellect or emotion, and the question of humility that is bound up with it, is one, as I have tried to show elsewhere, that involves an opposition not merely between Buddha and this or that Occidental philosopher, but between the Asiatic outlook on life in general and that which has tended to prevail in Europe. The granting of the primacy to intellect or mind, in any sense those terms have had since Anaxagoras, would seem to be incompatible with humility. It is a task of absorbing interest to trace the struggle between Christian voluntarism with its subordination of man in his natural self — including the intellect — to God's will, and a resurgent rationalism. In tracing a subject of this kind one becomes aware of a main problem in the spiritual life of the Occident to which I have already referred ; reason has repeatedly aspired to rise out of its due place and then the resulting reactions against its presumption have encouraged various forms of obscurantism.

Among the doctrines in which reason has thus aspired unduly, with a corresponding tendency of pride to prevail over humility, Stoicism stands preëminent : first, because many important modern philosophies — for example, those of Descartes, Spinoza, and Kant — have in their practical bearing on life and conduct much in common with Stoicism ; secondly, because misleading comparisons have been made between the Buddhist and the Stoic. The Buddhist reminds one of the Stoic by the severity of the self-control he inculcates, also by his self-reliant spirit. He relies, however, in this discipline, not, like the Stoic, upon a 'reason' supposed to coincide with the cosmic order, but upon a will that transcends it. Reliance upon this will gives the psychic equivalent of the Christian submission to the divine will, in other words, of humility. The Stoic is a monist ; the Buddhist is like the Christian, an uncompromising dualist. So far from 'accepting the universe' in the Stoic sense, he rejects so much of it that the alarmed Occidental is inclined to ask whether anything remains.

Practically the difference between monist and dualist converges upon the problem of evil. The Stoic is a theoretic optimist ; Buddha, though very untheoretic here as elsewhere, is extraordinarily insistent upon the fact of evil. 'This alone I have taught,' he says, 'sorrow and the release from sorrow.' Buddha's emphasis on sorrow may seem to some incompatible with the urbanity I have attributed to him ; for nothing is more contrary to the ur-

bane temper than absorption in a single idea.   He really
aims at wholeness, a type of wholeness that it is hard for
us to grasp because breadth is for us something to be
achieved expansively and even by an encyclopaedic ag-
gregation of parts ; whereas the wholeness at which Buddha aims is related in fact, as it is etymologically, to holiness and is the result of a concentration of the will.   To
define the quality of will that Buddha would have us put
forth psychologically — that is, by his own method — is to
go very far indeed in an understanding of his doctrine.

The modern man is normally, as the Germans phrase it,
a 'yes-sayer' and a 'becomer' and glories in the fact.   Buddha on the other hand is probably the chief of all the 'no-
sayers' ; specifically he says no to everything that is im-
plicated in the element of change even to the point of
defining the highest good as 'escape from the flux.' 'What
is not eternal,' he says, 'does not deserve to be looked on
with satisfaction.'   In his rejection of the transitory for
the eternal he is, as I have just remarked, neither metaphysical nor theological, but psychological.   One needs
only to take a glance at the four noble truths of Buddha
to perceive that his doctrine is in its genuine spirit a psychology of desire.   The four noble truths themselves
need to be interpreted in the light of the three 'characteris-
tics,' which, we are told, only a Buddha can properly
proclaim : namely, (1) the impermanence of all finite
things ; in this sense (2) their lack of 'soul' or their 'un-
reality' ; and therefore (3) their final unsatisfactoriness.
As one becomes aware of the fact of impermanence and
of its implications, one tends to substitute for the ignoble
craving for what is subject to corruption the noble craving
for the 'incomparable security of a Nirvāna free from
corruption.'

Buddha's attitude towards the 'soul,' it should be observed, differs decisively from that of the Vedantists in India and from the somewhat similar doctrine of Plato in the West. His objection to those who assert a soul and other similar entities is not metaphysical but practical : they are thereby led to think they have transcended the transitory when they have not done so and are thus lulled into a false security. Buddha can scarcely be regarded as an idealist in any sense the term has ever had in the Occident. He is not an idealist in the Platonic sense, in spite of numerous and important points of contact between his teaching and that of Plato, because of the central clash I have just indicated. Still less is he an idealist in the other two main senses of the word : he does not hope, like Rousseau and the sentimentalists, to unify life in terms of feeling ; nor again, after the fashion of philosophers like Hegel, to unify it in terms of intellect. The unification that Buddha seeks is to be achieved by the exercise of a certain quality of will that says no to the outgoing desires with a view to the substitution of the more permanent for the less permanent among these desires and finally to the escape from impermanence altogether. His assertion of this quality of will is positive and empirical to the last degree.

I have already tried to make clear that Buddha is not merely a great religious personality but a thinker so trenchant as to invite comparison with the chief figures in Occidental thought. An interesting comparison suggests itself at this point with the thinker who has had a preponderant influence on recent Occidental philosophy — Immanuel Kant. Anyone who glances through the three critiques of Kant will be struck by the phrase *a priori* which recurs innumerable times and gives the key to the whole body of doctrine. To Kant it seemed that a resort to some kind of *apriorism* was necessary if one was to bind together and unify the elements of experience that the empirical method of Hume seemed to dissolve into a flux of unrelated impressions. Buddha would have opposed Hume not on *apriorist* but empirical grounds. He would have asserted a quality of will peculiar to man not as a theory but as a fact, as one of the immediate data of consciousness. Buddha may be defined indeed, in contradistinction to a naturalistic empiricist like Hume, as a religious empiricist. One may perhaps best illustrate what it means to assert positively and critically a religious will in man by a study of Buddha's way of dealing with the three questions that must, according to Kant, confront every philosopher : What can I know ? What must I do ? What may I hope ?

In virtue of its intellectualist temper Western philosophy has always shown a strong predilection for the first of these questions, the so-called problem of knowledge. The drift of the modern philosophy of the West towards epistemological inquiry has been marked since Descartes. From the time of Locke one is tempted to define this philosophy as a long debauch of epistemology. The various subsidiary questions that have been discussed — the question of substance, of innate ideas, of causation, of time and space, both in themselves and in their relation to one another — all finally converge upon the question as to the relation of appearance to reality. This endless epistemological debate would be justified if it could be shown to have prepared the way for a more adequate reply to Kant's second question : What must I do ? The Christian supernaturalist would not, however, grant that it has. The false dualism set up by Descartes has been eliminated, he would admit, but he would add that the true dualism has been eliminated along with it — the opposition, namely, between God's will and man's. The Buddhist sets up a

similar opposition between a higher and a lower will, not,
however, on dogmatic but on psychological grounds.
Western thinkers from St. Augustine to William James
who have sought to deal with the will psychologically are
in agreement with one another and with Buddha in at least
one particular : will is revealed above all in the act of attention or concentration.   The office of a Buddha is to
proclaim the truths to which man must attend if he would
escape from sorrow.   The 'causal nexus' or 'chain of de-
pendent origination' that leads to the rise of sorrow is extraordinarily difficult to grasp.   To the Occidental indeed it is likely to seem a hopeless puzzle.   The essential
link in the chain is at all events 'ignorance.'   Strictly
speaking, one does not in the Buddhist sense overcome
ignorance merely by acquiescing in the four noble truths.
Anyone who does not get beyond this stage is compared
to a cowherd counting another's kine.   A man may possess the noble truths and so escape from sorrow only by
acting upon them.   Knowledge follows upon will.   The
term faith has had various meanings in Buddhism as in
Christianity.   The original meaning is faith to act.   In
so far, the Buddhist is in agreement with the Christian
voluntarist when he proclaims that we do not know in
order that we may believe, but we believe in order that we
may know.

In its primary emphasis on will, the doctrine of Buddha
is not a system in the Occidental sense but a 'path.'   A
Buddha is simply one who has trodden this path and can
report to others what he has found.   In this sense he is the
Tathāgata.   He who would tread the same path must not
be diverted from concentration on the goal by anything
to the right or to the left.   Everything is to be set aside
which does not, in Buddha's own phrase, make for 'qui-

escence, knowledge, supreme wisdom, and Nirvāna.' Anyone who entered the Buddhist order in the hope of finding a solution for his merely speculative difficulties was
doomed to disappointment.   We are told that one of the
brethren once came to Buddha with a list of such difficulties — for example, whether the world is finite or infinite,
eternal or not eternal, whether soul and body are one or
separate, whether the saint exists or does not exist after
death, etc. — and complained to him that he had received
no enlightenment on these points.   Buddha replied to him
in substance that human nature is sick of a disease.   His
own rôle he conceived to be that of the physician.   Anyone who refused to act on his teaching until he had an
answer to such questions Buddha compared to a man who
had been wounded by a poisoned arrow and was unwill-
ing to receive medical aid until he had learned whether
the man who had wounded him was of light or dark complexion, belonged to the Brahman or warrior caste, etc.
No one was ever more unfriendly than Buddha to persons
who had 'views.'   One must indeed agree with a German
student of Buddhism that the dislike of mere speculation
is the distinguishing mark of the authentic doctrine.   One
may, however, refuse to agree with him that this practical
and unmetaphysical temper is a weakness.   Some questions Buddha would dismiss because they are intrinsically
unthinkable ; others because they are not worthy of
thought — do not, in his own phrase, make for edification.
Among the questions that he thus dismisses are several
that have been persistently debated in Occidental religion
and philosophy.

   In defining the topics with which the man who has renounced the world may properly concern himself Buddha
makes a distinction similar to that of Christ between the

things of God and the things of Cæsar. So far from en-
couraging the members of his order to take a part in political life, he would not even have them discuss politics.

Though a Buddha may proclaim to those seeking to
enter the path the truths on which they may profitably
concentrate and at the same time set them a persuasive example, he is not to be regarded in the full Christian sense
as a Saviour. In the last analysis a man must, according
to Buddha, save himself. Though both Christian and
Buddhist associate salvation with the putting forth of a
similar quality of will, no small difference between the
two results from the fact that the Christian associates this
quality of will in a greater or lesser degree with divine
grace. He would even tend to regard as blasphemous
Buddha's dictum : 'Self is the lord of self. Who else can
be the lord ?' To be sure, Christians themselves have
varied widely in their views of grace. Some would receive the grace immediately, others mediately through the
Church. The Jansenist, for example, with his emphasis
on the inner light seems spiritually autonomous, at least so
far as outer authority is concerned, compared with the
Jesuit. But even the inner light of the Jansenist, imply-
ing as it does complete dependence on the divine will, is
something far removed from the spiritual autonomy of the
Buddhist, an autonomy so complete that in describing
it one is constrained to employ at the risk of grave misunderstanding the terms self-reliance and individualism ;
for in the West the doctrine of self-reliance, from the
ancient Cynics and Stoics down to Emerson, has been associated with pride rather than humility. The Buddhist
type of individualism again is at the opposite pole from
the type with which we are familiar nowadays — the type
which combines a gospel of self-expression with the eva-
sion of moral responsibility. Buddha seems to the Occi-

dental to allow insufficiently for self-expression, at the
same time that he gives the widest possible extension to
the doctrine that a man is simply reaping, in the good or
evil that befalls him, the fruits of his own sowing.   These
fruits seem even more inevitable than in Christianity, inas-
much as man is accountable to Law and not to a more or
less arbitrary and capricious divine will.   He cannot ascribe his failure to make the salutary effort to any denial
of grace nor can he look to a Saviour to do for him what
he is unable to do for himself.   He cannot, again, substitute for self-reliance a reliance upon rites and ceremonies,
a reliance reckoned by Buddha among the 'ten fetters.'
At the very end of his life Buddha exhorted his followers
to be 'refuges unto themselves.'   A still more individualistic flavour is given to such utterances by the positive and
critical element in Buddhistic teaching to which I have
already called attention.   Buddha would not have his followers receive spiritual truth merely on his own authority,
nor again on that of tradition.   As a result of the primary
emphasis on Law the temper of the Buddhist is more im-
personal than that of the Christian.   An effusion like Pascal's *Mystère de Jésus*, profoundly religious in its own
way, would have seemed to him to involve a morbid ex-
acerbation of personality.

A statement of this kind applies above all to the original
doctrine.   The spirit of passionate devotion (*bhakti*) that
developed in so striking a fashion in Hinduism has its
equivalent in later Buddhism.   In general much that I
have been saying would need to be modified or even ex-
actly reversed, if I were attempting an account of the
various forms of Mahāyāna.   Thus some of these forms
developed a confidence in rites and ceremonies as aids to
salvation that probably goes beyond anything of the kind
that has been witnessed in Christianity.   The example of

the prayer-mill will occur to everybody. Mahāyāna has again in many of its forms encouraged the very type of theosophic and metaphysical speculation that Buddha himself repudiated. A debate regarding the relation of appearance to reality was carried on for centuries in connexion with this movement which is probably at least equal in subtlety to corresponding epistemological inquiries in the Occident. To be sure Buddha was himself prodigiously subtle. This subtlety, unlike that of the Mahāyānist, was, however, psychological rather than metaphysical. Finally the spiritual autonomy or self-reliance encouraged by the original doctrine receives far less emphasis in Mahāyāna, and is at times abandoned entirely. In direct proportion to the completeness of this abandonment, Buddha ceases to be a man and becomes a god or saviour. The teaching of a higher will is retained, but is so modified as to approximate at times to the Christian doctrine of grace. The abandonment of spiritual self-reliance was often conscious and deliberate. According to the reasoning of certain Mahāyānists in Japan, men may formerly have been capable of achieving salvation by their own efforts, but, in view of their present degeneracy, their only hope is in the grace and mercy of Amitabha. At the same time debates arose between the partisans of grace and of good works (in the ritualistic sense) not unlike those which have gone on in certain periods of Christianity. Analogies of this kind are indeed so numerous that some have suspected a direct or indirect influence upon Mahāyāna of a distinctly gnostic type of Christianity. There is a sense, one should add, in which Buddhist believers of all types have been comparatively individualistic. They have not on the whole been submitted to a rigid outer authority. Above all the Buddhist world has never known any organization for enforcing outer authority comparable in elaborateness and effectiveness to the Roman Catholic Church, itself modeled in important respects on Roman imperial organization. One may sum up the whole subject by saying that though Mahāyāna and Hīnayāna have much in common in their strictly ethical teaching, Mahāyāna has tended to give to this teaching a radically different doctrinal setting.

Keeping this general contrast in mind we may return to Buddha's positive and psychological method of dealing with the problem of the will. In the contrast he establishes between the expansive desires and a will that is felt, with reference to these desires, as a will to refrain, he is, as I have said, an uncompromising dualist. By exercising this quality of will a man may gradually put aside what is impermanent in favour of what is more permanent and finally escape from impermanence altogether. The chief virtue for Buddha is therefore the putting forth of this quality of effort, spiritual strenuousness, as one may say. His last exhortation to his disciples was to practise this virtue (*appamāda*) unceasingly. Anyone who has grasped all that it implies has gone far in his understanding of the genuine doctrine.

We are told that the exposition by a Buddhist missionary of aphorisms on the importance of spiritual effort, similar no doubt in substance and possibly even in form to the second chapter of the present Dhammapada, led to the conversion of Asoka, an event of incalculable importance for the culture of the Far East. Asoka showed that he had caught the very spirit of the Sakya sage when he proclaimed to his subjects : 'Let all joy be in effort.' 'Let small and great exert themselves.' Asoka was active in every sense of the word ; so was Buddha himself for that matter, as should be sufficiently clear to anyone who considers the attention he must have given to details in the founding of his religious order. But, though Buddha and Asoka were men of action in every sense of the word, it goes without saying that they were less interested in outer than in inner action. Buddha brings all forms of work into relation with one another, asserting the final superiority of the form by which one wins to self-mastery. He develops the paradox of religion that the man who is outwardly idle may be at once more strenuously and more profitably employed than the man who is outwardly active. On one occasion a rich Brahman farmer to whom Buddha had presented himself for alms reproached him with being an idler. Buddha replied that he was engaged in an even more important form of tillage than that of the soil. 'Faith is the seed, penance the rain, understanding my yoke and plough, modesty the pole of the plough, mind the tie, thoughtfulness my ploughshare and goad . . . exertion my beast of burden.' As a result of this spiritual husbandry one achieves the 'fruit of immortality.' Everything indeed hinges upon the quality of one's working, whether one sets out to be a carpenter, a king, or a saint.

The term *Karma* (work), though sometimes used in much the same sense as *appamāda*, a term reserved for the salutary exercise of the higher will, is applied more commonly to the doctrine of the deed in general, to the affirmation in the widest possible sense that 'what we have been makes us what we are.' The belief in Karma in this extended sense with its correlative belief in reincarnation, was not, it is scarcely necessary to add, peculiar to Buddha. It has been all but universal in India from early times and has also appealed to important Western thinkers like Plato. However, according to the view of the orthodox Buddhist, the Master did not base his acceptance of Karma on traditional grounds but on immediate perception. To be sure the nature of the insight of a Buddha as well as the way in which Karma fulfills itself are both numbered among the 'unthinkables.' This much, at most, is certain, that the state of Buddhahood is conceived as a state of pure vision and that among the truths comprised in this vision is the truth that as a man sows even so he shall reap. A Buddha is supposed to be immediately aware not merely of his own Karma, but, at will, of the Karma of others. An ordinary Buddhist and even a non-Buddhist may acquire in some degree the supernormal memory that this type of vision implies, though their illumination in this particular is, we are told, compared with that of an Arhat Buddha, as the light of a candle compared with the blaze of the noonday sun. One may note in passing that as a result of the insistence on the accountability of the individual not merely for his conduct in his present life but for that of his remoter past, two ideas coalesce in Buddhism that have tended to fly apart in the West — the idea of sudden conversion and the idea of habit. Sudden conversion is admitted by the Buddhist, but is usually represented as the result of a long habituation. The impressions and acts that have been associated with these impressions, not merely in one's present brief span of life but in one's secular past, lie hidden in what the modern psychologist would term the unconscious, and tend to give a bias to one's character and conduct both now and in one's secular future. Karma thus envisaged is a sort of fate, but a fate of which a man is himself the author and which is not at any particular moment entirely subversive of moral freedom.

It is in their respective attitudes towards the unconscious that the difference between a genuine supernaturalist like Buddha and the primitivist is especially manifest.

The primitivist is ready to surrender to the swarming images of the unconscious at the expense both of his intellect and of his higher will, in the hope that he may thus enjoy a sense of creative spontaneity. Buddha, on the contrary would put the intellect, felt as a power of discrimination, in the service of the higher will. He holds that it is possible by this coöperation to explore the unconscious, uncovering and finally eradicating the secret germs that, if allowed to develop freely, will result in future misery. Insight, as Buddha understands it, is marked by an increasing awareness. It is at the opposite pole from the diffuse reverie that has been so encouraged by our modern return to nature. A man's wisdom is measured by the extent to which he has awakened from the dream of sense. Goethe is very Buddhistic when he says that error bears the same relation to truth that sleeping does to waking. The very word Buddha means the Awakened. 'Right awareness' is indeed the seventh stage of the Buddhist 'path,' immediately preceding the final stage of 'right meditation.'

We come here to what is for Buddha fundamental in religion. To many things that have been regarded as indispensable in other faiths — for example, prayer and belief in a personal deity — he grants a secondary place or even no place at all ; but without the act of recollection or spiritual concentration he holds that the religious life cannot subsist at all.

Certain scholars have tended to emphasize the relationship betwen the Samkhya and Yoga Philosophies and Buddhism. Too little is known, however, about the historical development of the Hindu philosophical systems to justify one in asserting any specific borrowings from them on the part of Buddha. Moreover, as I have already pointed out, Buddhism is in its true spirit not a philosophical system at all but a 'path.' If one takes, however, Yoga, not in its systematic but in its psychological sense, one is justified in affirming a deep kinship between it and Buddhist teaching. In this psychological sense India, from a period even far anterior to Buddha, has been dominated, — one is at times tempted to say, obsessed, — by the idea of Yoga. One will be helped in understanding this word by keeping in mind its etymology which relates it to the Latin *jugum* and our word yoke. Metaphorically a man practises Yoga when he yokes or reins in the impulses of the natural man, though the term is usually reserved for the putting forth of this special quality of will in meditation. The yoking of self in meditation is at times compared to the actual yoking of horses or oxen. Buddha himself is described with some justification in one of the later Buddhist writings as the great *yogi*. A religious teacher cannot be explained merely in terms of environment. He does, however, presuppose an immense previous development, the turning of the attention of a multitude of men in a given direction, in this case to the quality of will, by which man may transcend his natural self. In much the same way the appearance of a Darwin or a Pasteur is not explained by the primary concentration on the natural order that has been under way in the Occident for several centuries past ; it does, however, presuppose some such development. Buddha is supposed to have received from previous masters of Yoga an initiation into all the stages of meditation with the exception of the last or Nirvānic stage. This last stage is declared by Buddha, who is not in general friendly to absolutes and ultimates, to work that final emancipation from the transitory at which the whole doctrine aims. From this point of view Nirvāna has been the subject of much, and, as it seems to the Buddhist, unintelligent discussion in the Occident. As a rule, the Western student is repelled by Nirvāna, to which he gives a nihilistic interpretation, and at the same time is attracted by Buddha's compassionateness. Buddha taught a boundless love, it would appear, that had as its goal mere nothingness. One must, however, if one is to avoid grave misunderstanding, interpret both 'love' and Nirvāna with reference to the special quality of will put forth in meditation. As I have already said, this will is in all its aspects a will to refrain and in its more radical aspects a will to renounce. What the Buddhist renounces are the expansive desires. Nirvāna is, in its literal meaning, the going out or extinction of these desires — especially of the three fires of lust, ill-will, and delusion. The notion that what ensues upon this extinction is mere emptiness is not genuinely Buddhistic. The craving for extinction in the sense of annihilation or non-existence (*vibharatanhā*) is indeed expressly reprobated in the Buddhist writings. The Buddhist quest is at bottom not for mere cessation but for the eternal. Negatively Nirvāna is defined as 'escape from the flux,' positively as the 'immortal element.' Strictly speaking, what is above the flux cannot be defined in terms of the flux, and 'mind' is for Buddha an organ of the flux. Anyone therefore who demands at the outset a firm intellectual formulation of Nirvāna has, from the Buddhist point of view, missed the point. The notion of Nirvāna that one may get in this way has about as much value, to use an image that Buddha employs in a slightly different connexion, as the theories that a chick that has not broken its way through its shell might form of the outside world. The important fact is that the chick is able to peck its way through the shell ; even so, says Buddha, man has the power of will, if he would but exercise it, to tread the path and achieve its fruition. If one inquire as to the nature of this fruition one is simply told that the saint can no longer be confined in the categories of ordinary consciousness ; he has become 'deep, immeasurable, unfathomable like the mighty ocean.'

Though the nature of this fruition cannot be defined abstractly it can to some extent be described psychologically and concretely ; all the more so in that Nirvāna is normally attained in the present life. According to Pascal, those alone deserve commendation who have succeeded in combining properly a sense of man's grandeur with a sense of his misery. Buddha seems to deserve this commendation, though his way of conceiving of man's grandeur in particular is not altogether in consonance with Christianity. This grandeur consists in the fact that the Buddhas appear as men and that the human state is in general more favourable than any other to the attainment of sanctity. Not merely Buddha himself, but many of his followers are supposed to have achieved Nirvāna and to have been in a position to compare this experience with what may be experienced in ordinary consciousness. We have already seen that Buddha subordinated the first of Kant's three questions, 'What can I know ?', to the second, 'What must I do ?' A similar subordination appears in his answer to the third question, 'What may I hope ?' In a verse of doubtful syntax, Pope has told us that man never is but always to be blessed. Buddha, on the contrary, aims at a present blessedness and does not encourage one to entertain any hope that is likely to divert one from this blessedness and the kind of effort by which it is attained. It goes without saying that he did not cherish the humanitarian hope : he did not, like the youthful Wordsworth, make 'society his glittering bride,' or like Tennyson look forward to a 'far-off divine event.' He was free from the nostalgic longing, the vague out-reaching of the imagination with which this type of hope has been so often associated. Compared with that perfect emancipation of the spirit at which he aims, even the older form of hope, that of bliss in a world to come, is deemed unworthy of the true disciple:

> The strong gods pine for my abode,
> And pine for me the sacred seven :
> But thou, meek lover of the good,
> Find me and turn thy back on heaven.

One should add that the 'Nirvāna here and now' (*Samditthakam Nibbanam*) of the Buddhist has much in common with the 'release in this life,' (*jivan-mukti*) of the Hindu philosopher. One may, however, affirm confidently that no religious teacher was ever more opposed than Buddha in his scheme of salvation to every form of postponement and procrastination. He would have his followers take the cash and let the credit go — though the cash in this case is not the immediate pleasure but the immediate peace.

The peace in which the doctrine culminates is not, the Buddhist would insist, inert but active, a rest that comes through striving. In general the state that supervenes upon the turning away from the desires of the natural man is not, if one is to believe the Buddhist, a state of cool disillusion. One may apply to it, indeed, the term enthusiasm, though the enthusiasm is not of the emotional type with which we are so familiar, but rather of the type which has been defined as 'exalted peace.' Buddha himself seems to speak from an immeasurable depth of calm, a calm that is without the slightest trace of languor. The innumerable images of the founder of the faith scattered throughout the Far East strive to render this effect of meditative tranquillity, at times, as in the great Buddha of

Kamakura in Japan,* with notable success. Anyone who like Buddha does not indulge 'the desire of the moth for the star,' and the psychic restlessness that it encourages, is likely to seem to an Occident permeated with romanticism to lack not merely poetry but religion. Mr. Chesterton, for example, seeks to prove, from this point of view, the superiority of the Christian over the Buddhist saint. 'The Buddhist saint,' he says, 'always has his eyes shut, while the Christian saint always has them very wide open. The Buddhist saint has a sleek and harmonious body, but his eyes are heavy and sealed with sleep. The mediaeval saint's body is wasted to its crazy bones, but his eyes are frightfully alive. The Buddhist is looking with peculiar intentness inwards. The Christian is staring with frantic intentness outwards,' etc. There are no doubt saints and saints. The London papers published a few years ago the following dispatch from India: 'A new saint has appeared in the Swāt Valley. The police are after him.' But a saint, whether Buddhist or Christian, who knows his business as a saint is rightly meditative and in proportion to the rightness of his meditation is the depth of his peace. We have it on an authority which Mr. Chesterton is bound to respect that the kingdom of heaven is within us. It would be interesting to hear Mr. Chesterton explain how a saint can find that which is within by 'staring frantically outwards.' Failing like many others to discriminate between romanticism and religion, Mr. Chesterton has managed to misrepresent both Buddhism and Christianity. The truth is, that though Christianity from the start was more emotional in its temper than Buddhism, and though an element of nostalgia entered into it from an early period, it is at one in its final emphasis with the older religion. In both faiths this emphasis is on the peace that passeth understanding.

* Strictly speaking this is an image, not of Gotama but of Amitabha Buddha.

Matthew Arnold is therefore infelicitous from both a Christian and a Buddhist point of view in defining religion merely as morality touched by emotion. The numerous persons who have seen in the original teaching of Buddha in particular only the ethical element have been guilty of grave misapprehension. The path to religion leads through morality — on this point Buddha is most explicit ; but as one approaches the goal one enters into an entirely different element : the saint who has attained the Nirvānic calm is, we are told repeatedly, 'beyond good and evil.'

The confusion regarding the relation of religion in general and Buddhism in particular to emotion is still more serious. The Western student, I have said, is likely to be repelled by Nirvāna but is almost invariably attracted by the prominence Buddha gives to love or compassion. It is not as a matter of fact easy to over-emphasize this side of his teaching. 'The boundless good-will' that he urges us to cultivate, 'even as a mother at the risk of her life watches over her own child, her only child,' embraces not only man but the whole animate world. Buddhist love can, however, like Nirvāna, be understood only in connexion with the special form of activity that is put forth in meditation. It does not well forth spontaneously from the natural man but is, like Christian charity, the supernatural virtue *par excellence*. The current confusion on this point is perhaps the most striking outcome of the sentimentalism of the eighteenth century and of the emotional romanticism of the nineteenth century that prolonged it. This confusion may be defined psychologically as a tendency to substitute for a superrational concentration of will a subrational expansion of feeling. How many persons, for example, exalt the 'love' of St. Francis who, in their total outlook on life, are almost inconceivably remote from the humility, chastity, and poverty from which, in the eyes of

St. Francis himself, the love was inseparable ! The emotionalists have been busy with even more august figures than St. Francis, for example with Christ himself. They have also inclined, although this tendency is less familiar, to interpret Buddha subrationally. The latter tendency is probably best exemplified in Schopenhauer who founds ethics upon a distinctly subrational sympathy (or pity) and then proceeds to associate this type of sympathy with Buddha and with the wisdom of the East in general. Schopenhauer knew little about the authentic teaching of Buddha, but his error is so fundamental that it is doubtful whether he would have corrected it even if he had been more adequately informed.

The real Buddha, I have tried to make clear, though an enthusiast, was not an emotionalist. For the Buddhist, emotion, like morality, lies on the way to religion ; but as one approaches the goal one enters, as I have said, into a different element — an element of unalloyed calm. It would never have occurred to Buddha and his early followers to measure a man's humanity, much less his religion by his 'droppings of warm tears.' The tears shed by Ananda, the favourite disciple, on learning from the Master of his approaching end, tears that seem to us so touching, were regarded by the Arhats or true saints as a mark of his spiritual immaturity. They had been so schooled in the truths of impermanence that they were not to be shaken even by the passing of a Buddha. A religious peace so perfect as this seems to us to exclude tenderness to a degree that is slightly inhuman. For the Buddhist, however, the peace and a love that has grown 'great' and 'immeasurable,' have a common source — namely, a right use of meditation.

Moreover one should not forget that though Buddha was very pitiful, he was also very stern. His love is not of the kind that is subversive of justice. In the case of Buddha, as in that of Christ, love and justice seem to be so perfectly harmonized as to constitute but a single virtue. Later in both Buddhism and Christianity, the principle of compassion tends to get divorced, in some degree at least, from justice. The cult of the goddess of mercy in Mahāyāna lands has certain analogies with the cult of the Virgin in the West. The sympathy of the modern humanitarian, though it also tends to override justice, and though it has also, as I have already said, been frequently associated with Christ or Buddha, needs to be judged rather differently — as something more unmistakably subrational.

By its predominant emphasis on the will to refrain, Buddhism is likely to seem to the Occidental unduly negative. The peace and all-embracing charity that the saint is supposed to attain can, however, scarcely be regarded as merely negative. Moreover, though the fruit of the doctrine is often presented negatively as 'release from sorrow,' it is also presented positively as happiness. The Buddhist temper, like that of the Christian and unlike that of the Stoic, is cheerful. Rhys Davids, who spent a life-time in contact with the original documents, insists on the 'exuberant optimism' of the early Buddhists. The phrase would seem to call for some qualification. The true Buddhist, like the true Christian, takes a gloomy view of the unconverted man ; but, though holding that life quantitatively is bad, he is, regarding a certain quality of life, unmistakably buoyant. Joy rightly receives due emphasis in St. Paul's admirable list of the fruits of the spirit. The same virtue appears in the equivalent lists proclaimed by Asoka to his subjects : the joy in both cases arises from an exercise of the will to refrain. The early members of the Buddhist Order at all events were not unfamiliar with what Pascal terms total and blissful renunciation (*renonciation totale et douce*). 'Let us live happily, then, though we call nothing our own !' Buddhism, indeed, at least in its original form, is more frankly eudaemonistic than Christianity. Traditionally the motive suggested to the Christian for renouncing the world has been the love of God. Buddha would have one make a similar renunciation with an eye primarily to one's own advantage. The phrase 'enlightened self-interest' has come to have unfortunate connotations. The meaning given to 'enlightened' and 'self-interest' by Buddha is at all events at a wide remove from the meaning given to the same terms by the utilitarian. Aristotle is nearer to Buddha when he counsels a man to be a true lover of himself. Doctrines that urge one not to think of one's self at all but to act purely for the love or greater glory of God, or in more recent times, purely for the love of humanity, have a certain abstract nobility ; but it may be doubted whether they are as deeply grounded as the doctrine of true self-love in the facts of human nature. To be sure, the doctrine of true self-love, like any other doctrine that may be set up, is easily abused. We hear of the prevalence in Buddhist lands of a literal and unimaginative computation of merits and demerits according to the law of Karma, a sort of spiritual book-keeping that may lead one to be self-regarding in the wrong sense. The complaint is also made that, as a result of Buddha's insistence that a man's first duty is to himself, Buddhists are, as compared with Christians, lacking in the spirit of mutual helpfulness.

It is hard to see why the teaching of self-love should result thus undesirably, if it is made sufficiently plain that the self that one loves is not only a higher self, but a self that one possesses in common with other men. As for the ordinary, or natural self, Buddha often uses language that reminds one of Christianity. His paradox of true self-love, interpreted in the light of renunciation, does not turn out so very differently from the Christian paradox of dying that one may

live.   According to Buddha, anything that is impermanent
is not only unreal but finally illusory.   In virtue of his psychological method, however, he does not as a rule dwell,
after the fashion of the Hindu philosopher, on illusion in
general (*māyā*) but on conceit or the illusion of the ego
(*manas*).   The eliminations imposed by the putting aside
of the false or illusory self are, even from the point of view
of the austere Christian, extremely drastic.   Failure to
make these eliminations is due to a failure to exercise the
higher will, the will to refrain.   One may say indeed that,
according to Buddha, the root diseases of human nature
are conceit and indolence, and that the conceit itself turns
out at last to be only an aspect of the indolence ; so that,
even as spiritual strenuousness is the supreme Buddhist virtue, so spiritual slackness or supineness is the unpardonable
offence.   One must constantly keep in mind, however, that
both the strenuousness and its opposite have reference primarily, not to the outer world, but to meditation.   'Meditate therefore,' says Buddha, 'and be not indolent lest later
ye have reason to repent.'

Meditation is, indeed, so paramount in Buddhist belief
and is carried so far that one is forced to consider in connexion with it one of the most difficult of all questions —
that of mysticism.   The first step in dealing with this baf-
fling term would seem to be to limit it.   The tendency on
the part of certain authorities so to widen the term as to
make it identical with religion itself is inadmissible.   Bos-
suet, for example, although genuinely religious, was, so far
from being mystical, positively unfriendly to mysticism.
One is aided in dealing with the word mystic, as in dealing
with *yoga*, by a reference to its etymology.   Etymologically the mystical state implies an actual closing of the
eyes.   In the true mystic there is always a considerable
blunting and even complete suppression of ordinary con-

sciousness in favour of what is conceived to be a wholeness of some kind or a more genuine unity.   Buddhist meditation is undoubtedly mystical in this sense.   For example, we learn regarding Buddha himself the realistic detail that on a certain occasion he was not disturbed in his contemplation by a thunderbolt that struck near him, killing two peasants and four oxen.   One is reminded of the *henôsis* or mystic absorption in the One of a Plotinus.   Yet right at this point one needs to make sharp discriminations.   The teaching of Plotinus and the neo-Platonists in general, however much it may agree with that of Buddha in this or that particular, is in its total tendency, radically divergent. This divergence is nowhere more apparent than in the quality of the mysticism the two teachings have fostered. On the immensity of the neo-Platonic influence, especially of Plotinus, not merely on European culture but on the culture of the Near East, it is scarcely necessary to dilate. Through the treatise of the pseudo-Dionysius and other channels this influence penetrated into Christianity itself. It received a fresh impetus in the early Renaissance from such works as Ficino's commentary on the 'Symposium.' The confusion between the neo-Platonic interpretation of Plato and a genuine Platonism has not been dissipated even to the present day.   It is possible to detect the persistent neo-Platonic strain in mystics so far apart in time as Eckhardt, Boehme, and Blake.

The first obvious contrast between Buddha and the mystics who have been in greater or lesser degree neo-Platonic, appears in their respective attitudes towards the problem of evil.   For Plotinus evil has no intrinsic reality, it is only an absence of the good.   One may recognize in Plotinus himself an element of genuine spirituality — he is very far from being like Buddha a clear-cut figure — and one may at the same time insist on the danger of this notion that evil is mere deprivation. It tends to discredit everything that is felt negatively and restrictively, to associate the pursuit of the good with expansive longing rather than with renunciation. The nostalgia that has assumed so many forms in Western religion and literature is not unrelated to the neo-Platonic influence. The reaching out towards the 'infinite' in this sense is at all events alien to a teacher who held that the higher will in man is primarily an inhibition, and who is in this sense, as I have said, an uncompromising dualist.

The true humility of the Christian with its subordination of man in his natural self to a divine will is also sharply dualistic. The mystic of the neo-Platonic type tends, on the contrary, to blunt the edge of this dualism or even to suppress it entirely. He is less concerned than the Christian with man's sinfulness or than the Buddhist with his spiritual indolence felt as a positive evil. With the resulting decline in humility, he is inclined to substitute for the sense of one's dependence on the divine an assertion of identity with it. The Roman Catholic Church has given recognition to mystics who exhibit traits that to the ordinary person seem pathological. It may be doubted, however, whether with its secular experience it has ever countenanced any mystic capable of announcing, as Sister Katrei announced to Eckhardt, that she had 'become God.'

Eckhardt's own mysticism has, along with marked neo-Platonic elements, points of contact with the mediaeval school that exalted intellect above will. In general it is important to determine the attitude of a mystic towards intellect both in itself and in its relation to will. The neo-Platonic mystic reminds one of the Buddhist in that his ultimate is an indefinable. The Buddhist holds, however, that in order to achieve his ultimate he needs to exercise the sharpest discrimination. One is tempted to say, although the phraseology is not Buddhistic, that in treading his 'path,' he would use his intellect as an instrument of the higher will. The neo-Platonist, on the contrary, tends to fall away from the form of concentration that seems so salutary to the Buddhist, in favour of expansiveness. He then wins a more or less mystical unity at the expense of discrimination. The maxim *omnis determinatio est negatio* is sound in itself. When, however, negation is conceived neo-Platonically as mere absence of the good, an interpretation of the maxim follows that is not conducive to self-limitation or to limitation of any kind. It is at all events highly important to know whether the union with a larger whole — the goal of every mystic — is won by the multiplication or the obliteration of distinctions. The intellect when left to its own devices is prone, as one may already see in Plotinus, to forget its secondary and instrumental rôle and to set up absolutes or, what amounts to the same thing, to devise some metaphysical denial of that dualism which is the scandal of reason and is nevertheless one of the immediate data of consciousness. This monistic trend, even when it does not take on a mystical colouring, results in its extreme form, and that from the Taoists of ancient China down to Hegel and Croce, in the assertion of a *coincidentia oppositorum* or identity of contradictories, and finally to a denial of the distinction that it would seem most important to preserve — that between good and evil. The intellectual running together of opposites has, as every student of our modern 'return to nature' is aware, its emotional equivalent, which also frequently takes on a mystical colouring. Mysticism of this latter type would seem to be at the opposite pole from that of Buddha. The early Buddhists practised certain 'unpleasant meditations' on the decay and corruption of the body which will be found to justify their title. One may cite by way of contrast the utterance of the 'mystic' Novalis: 'One touches heaven when one touches a human body' ; or the somewhat grotesque equivalent of this utterance in Walt Whitman, who has also been termed a mystic : 'I dote on myself, there is that lot of me and all so luscious.' When Whitman speaks of the 'mystical deliria' of the senses he uses the word mystical in a sense, one scarcely need point out, that would have seemed to Buddha sheer madness. The primitivistic revery that is at the basis of the mysticism of a Novalis or a Whitman cannot, like genuine meditation, be regarded as a form of action. It results rather from a dissipation of attention, a relaxation of one's grip on the world of spiritual values and even on the facts of the natural order ; so much so at times as to suggest that it has its source in actual physical debility.

The foregoing analysis, if correct, would seem to justify the conclusion that the record of so-called mysticism in the Occident has been in general highly dubious ; that the modern return to nature in particular, though it has revealed new sources of poetry, offers in its mystical aspects, and that from either a Christian or a Buddhist point of view, a mere subrational parody of genuine meditation. It is well to remember that the Far East has also had a primitivistic movement of immense extent in Taoism and that, either as a result of Taoist intrusion or other influences, the Mahā-yānist seems to have developed at times a quality of meditation more or less pantheistic and in so far unlike that found in the original doctrine. Anyone who seeks to meditate in Buddha's sense must be, as regards the intellect, keenly discriminating, and, as regards the higher will, strenuous ; whereas according to Wordsworth, in what one is tempted to call his Taoist phase, the man who wishes to commune with nature must combine passivity with a distrust of the 'meddling intellect.'

In this matter of meditation as in other respects one scarcely needs to insist on the immensity of the psychic gap

that separates the Buddhist Orient from the Occident of
today. It is because of this gap, at least as much as because
of insufficient information, that so many Western treatises
on Buddhism are almost unconsciously partisan, at times
violently partisan. Renan maintained that one could not
be polite in a Parisian omnibus without violating the rules
of the company. Even so anyone who sets out to be a
Buddhist today would find himself in conflict with some
of the underlying assumptions of our civilization. An Occidental is as likely to be as much disconcerted on a first
reading of the Buddhist *Nikāyas* as one may suppose an
ancient Buddhist would be if set down in a modern power-
house. The phenomenal world that alone seems to us
real and to which we therefore cling desperately he would
have us look upon as a flying mist of illusion. On the other
hand the Nirvāna towards which Buddha urges us to strive
affects us as mere nothingness. It is to be feared that he
would have held our opinions on this point in scant esteem.
The truth of his discipline, he would have insisted, can be
apprehended only by putting it into practice. Knowledge in matters religious waits upon will. It is the result
of doing certain things. So far from doing these things,
we are doing almost the exact opposite. He would therefore have dismissed us as mere theorists. In general, it
may be a help in elucidating this subject to reverse the usual
question as to what we are to think of Buddha and ask
rather what Buddha would think of us. This latter question is one that can be answered with certainty, assuming
that Buddha remained Buddha and was not swept off his
feet by our wonderfulness ; for we are very wonderful.
The Oriental even at the present day is astounded by our
material achievements.

In its essence Buddhism is, as I have said, a psychology
of desire, so that all that is needed for a reply to the question

what Buddha would think of us is to compare positively and critically our attitude towards the expansive desires with that of Buddha.   The movement that became predominant in the Occident with the emergence of the middle class in the eighteenth century and which still continues, may be defined in its two main aspects as utilitarian and sentimental.   The outstanding characteristic of the movement in both of these aspects has been its enormous expansiveness.   The utilitarian is wont to pursue an ever expanding production as an end in itself.   The point of view of an eminent American economist has been summed up in the formula : 'Pigs for more pigs for more pigs.'   A world of frenzied producers requires as its complement a world of frenzied consumers.   The expert in advertising has been gravely praised of late for making two desires grow where only one grew before.   The extirpation of desire in the Buddhist sense, or even the limitation of desire in the humanistic sense, would plainly be injurious to trade. If need is felt of a counterpoise to the acquisitive life, recourse is had, not to a genuinely restrictive principle but to the sympathy and spirit of service recommended by the sentimentalists, which is at bottom only another form of expansion.   To both types of expansionist I have been defining, Buddha's psychology of desire seems intolerably astringent.   To Buddha, on the other hand, a view of life that combines the extreme of outer activity with the extreme of spiritual indolence would have seemed one-sided to the point of madness.   The current notion that it is possible to establish a collective peace and brotherhood among men who are individually filled with every manner of restlessness, would have seemed to him positively delirious.   We are wont to deal with the question of war and peace at its extreme periphery, — for example war or peace between nations.   Like the Christian, the Buddhist would begin at the centre — with the issue of war or peace in the heart of the individual.   Any conquest that the individual may win over his own inordinate desires will be reflected at once in his contact with other men.   If the individual happens to be one in high station, such a conquest may have almost immediate consequences in the field of political action.   One may illustrate interestingly from the history of Buddhism.   About 273 B.C., Asoka, grandson of that Chandragupta who defeated in the Punjab and drove back the Macedonian garrisons left by Alexander the Great, succeeded to a realm more extensive than modern British India.   He had it in his power to drench the world in blood.   He actually made a beginning — and then came his conversion to Buddhism.   The result may be told in his own words as they appear in the edicts which he caused to be engraved on rocks or pillars throughout his vast empire.   In one of his rock edicts he tells of his 'profound sorrow' at the hundreds of thousands who had been slain in his war on the Kalingas, as well as at the misery that had been brought upon a multitude of non-combatants. 'If a hundredth or a thousandth part of these were now to suffer the same fate it would be a matter of regret to his Majesty.'   A mighty emperor who not only repented of his lust of dominion but had his repentance cut into the rock for the instruction of future ages — this under existing circumstances is something to ponder on.   The type of statesman with whom we are familiar in these latter days is wont to indulge his own will to power as well as that of the national group to which he belongs, and then, when the untoward consequences appear, to evade responsibility. Nearly everyone, for example, who was concerned with the outbreak of the Great War has been proclaiming his own blamelessness and at the same time pointing an accusing finger at someone else.   We shall discover perhaps even

more unedifying aspects of human nature than this search
for scapegoats if we probe this whole question of war and
peace by a Buddhistic method ; if, in other words, we en-
visage it from the point of view of the inner life and then
deal with the inner life itself positively and critically, in
the opposition it offers between the principle of control and
the expansive desires.   According to an ancient Sanskrit
epigram the uncultivated man and the thoroughly cultivated man are alike in having few and simple desires ; the
man who has reached the stage of half-way knowledge, on
the other hand, is insatiable.   Precisely this type of in-
satiableness has appeared in the modern man who has become too critical to accept the traditional controls but not
critical enough to achieve new ones.   In tracing the process by which in our modern period the principle of control
in human nature has been weakened in favour of a sheer
expansiveness one needs to attend carefully to the fortunes
of the doctrine with which this principle had been traditionally associated — the doctrine of divine grace.   An important aspect of the sentimental movement has been prim-
itivism.   The primitivist inclines to look for goodness not
to the grace of God but to the grace of nature.   Instead
of the inner workings of the spirit on which both Christian
and Buddhist put so much emphasis, he proclaims a 'wise
passiveness.'   The utilitarian, representing the other chief
aspect of the modern movement, has obscured the truths
of the higher will in the Christian or any other form, by
his tendency to transfer action from the inner life to the
outer world, to put a material in place of a spiritual efficiency.   One can trace this development with special clear-
ness among Protestants, notably perhaps among Calvinists.
Calvin granted to God so much and to man so little in his
scheme of salvation that his followers inclined to turn their
efforts from the inner life where they seemed to be of no

avail to the outer world, and then, in the type of prosperity achieved by this kind of working, to see a sign that they were in the divine favour.   This development has rightly received attention from those who have studied the rise of modern capitalism with its exaltation of the acquisitive life.

At all events, an outstanding feature of the humanitarian movement on both its utilitarian and its sentimental side has been its expansiveness, its reaching out for more and ever for more.   The representatives of this movement are not willing to admit that they are foregoing the benefits that not merely Buddha but the religious and humanistic teachers of the Occident as well have associated, not with expansion, but with concentration.   On the contrary they have proclaimed a progress that is supposed to lead in the direction of peace and fraternal union among men.   In short, though resolved to renounce nothing, they hope to enjoy all the fruits of renunciation.   They would seem to illustrate, on a large, perhaps an unprecedented scale, a trait that is universally human but is specially visible in the half-educated man — the proneness namely to harbour desires that are not only numerous but often incompatible.   The explanation of this tendency to reach out after certain ends and at the same time seek to evade the means is only too obvious : though the ends are desirable the means are difficult and disciplinary.   The readiness of men to succumb to schemes for acquiring sudden wealth is familiar.   It probably offers only a faint image of their proneness to yield to the lure of teaching that seems to hold out the hope of spiritual riches without any corresponding effort.   In America — and America is the paradise of the half-educated — substantial material rewards await anyone who can devise some new and painless plan for getting 'in tune with the infinite.'

The revolution in the very basis of ethics implied in the

setting up of utilitarian or sentimental substitutes for religion has not perhaps attracted an amount of attention commensurate with its importance. The gravity of this revolution would probably have been more manifest had it not been accompanied by a sort of revolution in the dictionary. The words that had been used traditionally to sum up certain ethical and religious ideas were retained but with a modification of the traditional meanings. The modern movement indeed, especially since the eighteenth century, illustrates another trait of the imperfectly cultivated man : he not only has numerous and frequently incompatible desires, but he dissimulates this incompatibility both from himself and others by a vague and confused use of general terms, or it may be, by a transfer of general terms from one scheme of values to another. For example, the sentimentalist has associated words like virtue and conscience not, as traditionally, with a will to refrain, but with expansive emotion. The utilitarian again has also inclined to eliminate the will to refrain and the inner effort it involves in favour of a mere outer working. This shifting of emphasis is reflected above all in the changed meaning of the word comfort. Material comfort has come more and more to seem to the modern man a satisfying substitute for spiritual comfort. To be sure, one does not know what secret qualms may torture the modern man or at least an occasional modern man as he is whirled he knows not whither in an ever-increasing mass of interlocking machinery. To all outer appearances, however, most men no longer crave the security and serenity which are of the essence of religious comfort and have allowed these terms, like the term comfort itself, to be appropriated by the utilitarians. An American life insurance company recently advertised as follows : 'Buddha, who was born a prince, gave up his name, succession and his heritage to attain se-

curity. But . . . we do not have to give up the world ;
we have only to see a life insurance agent who can sell us
security for the future, the most direct step to serenity of
mind.'

The issues raised by this advertisement evidently involve
much more than one's attitude towards Buddha. For
example, the differences of outlook between Christ and
Buddha are inconsequential compared with the difference
between them both and the man who believes that serenity
and security are something one may purchase from the
agent of a life insurance company. In general, a collateral
benefit of any comprehension one may achieve of Buddha
is that it will help one to a better understanding of Christ.
One will be less likely to confound him with the humanitarian phantom that has for several generations past tended
to usurp his place. This usurpation has been made plau-
sible, as I have said, by a tampering with general terms ; it
has also illustrated on a large scale another human proclivity — the proclivity namely to read one's self into the
great figures of the past. Thus both primitivists and utilitarians have sought to refashion Christ in their own image.
For instance the author of a recent Life of Christ, Giovanni
Papini, complains that the 'exhausting mercantile supersti-
tion of our day' has led to an utterly one-sided activity.
The desirable opposite of this utilitarian one-sidedness is,
he would have us believe, not another form of action but
the sheer inaction (*Wu wei*) of the ancient Chinese Taoist,
which he proceeds to identify not merely with the primi-
tivism of Rousseau but also with the wisdom of Christ. On
the other hand, another recent interpreter of the Gospel
narrative, Mr. Bruce Barton, wishing to commend Christ
to an age that plumes itself above all on its efficiency, pre-
sents him as a master of the art of advertising and an an-
cestor of the modern man of business.

If the man of the West has been falling away from religion in the fashion I have indicated, it is not to be supposed that the man of the East has maintained himself on the level of religious insight that one finds in Buddha and his early followers. On the contrary, it would probably be even more difficult to find an *arhat* in the full Buddhist sense in contemporary Asia than it would be to discover any complete exemplar of Christian sanctity in the Occident. Furthermore, if we are to trust certain passages in the Pāli Canon, Buddha's own contemporaries, who were as definitely concentrating on religious problems as the present age is on material efficiency, did not find his teaching easy to grasp. 'Profound, O Vaccha, is this doctrine,' Buddha is represented as replying to a puzzled inquirer, 'recondite and difficult of comprehension, good, excellent and not to be reached by mere reasoning, subtle and intelligible only to the wise ; and it is a hard doctrine for you to learn who belong to another sect . . . and sit at the feet of another teacher.' There is also the tradition of the 'private Buddhas' who did not see fit to give their wisdom to the world. Nay, it is related of Gotama himself that, after having attained supreme illumination, he hesitated about attempting to bestow it upon mankind 'held spellbound by its lusts.' Finally Brahmā Sahampati himself appeared before him and entreated him not to disappear from the world without proclaiming the Doctrine. 'There are those,' he added, 'who will understand.' Buddha finally assented, exclaiming : 'The door is open to the deathless.'

If it was not easy for Buddha's contemporaries to enter the door thus opened, to attune their ears to 'sweet airs breathed from far past Indra's sky,' the task is doubly difficult for the unmeditative Occidental ; for it is plain that one cannot have even an inkling of the nature of the insight Buddha professed without some grasp on the idea of meditation. From this point of view the Occidental is likely to find the Buddha of certain schools of Mahāyāna more accessible, Buddha conceived less as a master of meditation than as a Lord of compassion ; such a conception, however, finds comparatively little support in the older records. To be sure, the Mahāyānist, even though he grant the greater historical authenticity of the Pāli Canon, is prone, like certain Christians, to take refuge in a theory of development and to allege in particular the paramount place given to compassion as proof of the superiority of the developed over the original doctrine. Theories of development are, however, when applied to religion, dubious, whether the religion be Buddhism or Christianity. Peripheral development there may well be — for example, in Buddhist or Christian art ; but development at the centre is another matter. A great religion is above all a great example ; the example tends to grow faint in time or even to suffer alteration into something very different. Buddhism seems to have most vitality today in Hīnayāna rather than in Mahāyāna lands. The reason may be that in the former lands there has been less sophistication of the figure of the Founder.

The whole question is related to a topic that is now being actively discussed : namely, what is the specifically Oriental element in the Orient and what should be the attitude of the Occident towards this element ? According to a recent French writer, Europe, appalled at the one-sided American cult of mass production and mechanical efficiency, feels that it may finally have to choose between Henry Ford and Gandhi. There is much in the teaching of Gandhi, however, that is more suggestive of Tolstoy than of the genuine Oriental seer. Buddha, on the other hand, not only stands for an idea that is typically, though not exclusively, Asiatic — the idea of meditation — but he deals with meditation and the form of effort it requires in a more positive and critical fashion perhaps than any other religious teacher. The significance of his teaching for the Occident, so far as it has any, would seem to be here. The scientific naturalists profess at present to have a monopoly of positive and critical method. The attempt, however, to bring the whole of human experience under the natural law, so far from being genuinely positive and critical, involves a lapse at some point into mere dogma and metaphysical assumption. It would seem desirable, then, that those who object on either humanistic or religious grounds to the over-reaching attitude of the scientific naturalists should not burden themselves with any unnecessary metaphysical or theological baggage, and that their appeal should be to experience rather than to some counter-dogma. As is well known, the more thorough-going naturalists have been tending more and more to discard speculative philosophy in favour of psychology ; and herein they are at one with Buddha. One is conscious, however, of some underlying discrepancy between Buddha and the naturalistic psychologists, and that precisely at the point where, in spite of serious divergences, these psychologists are in accord with one another. One may illustrate from the behaviourists and the psycho-analysts, who may be taken to represent the extreme opposing wings of contemporary psychology. The psycho-analyst is introspective, at least to the extent that he is concerned with certain desires and impulses of the natural man as reflected in states of consciousness. The behaviourist, on the other hand, is so eager to be 'objective,' to avoid even the suspicion of introspection, that he is ready to deny instinct as understood by the psycho-analyst and even consciousness itself. There is a sense in which Buddha agrees with both behaviourist and psycho-analyst. Like the psycho-analyst he reduces the human problem to a psychology of desire, and then deals with desire itself in terms of conflict and adjustment. Like the behaviourist, again, he would deal with man neither metaphysically nor theologically but positively, and from this point of view is ready to assert that 'man is what he does.' If in his total position he seems so widely removed from both psycho-analyst and behaviourist, the explanation is that he affirms as a matter of immediate perception a principle of control in man that all schools of naturalistic psychology deny in favour of some form of monism. If the quality of will proclaimed by Buddha and other religious teachers is a fact, it is plainly a fact of overwhelming importance ; so much so that any view of life that fails to reckon with it will finally turn out to be nugatory. If one affirms that man is what he does and then, like the behaviourist, conceives of doing merely in terms of reactions to outer stimuli, the result is a monstrous mutilation of human nature. A similar failure to take account of the higher will vitiates the psycho-analytical idea of adjustment. Religion also looks upon life as a process of adjustment. This process as envisaged by the Christian is summed up once for all in Dante's phrase : 'His will is our peace.' A reading of works like the Dhammapada suggests that the psychological equivalent of this form of adjustment was not unknown to the Buddhist.

It is true that in a naturalistic era like the present the refusal to recognize a super-rational factor in human nature has a certain plausibility. At such a time a psychology that does not discriminate qualitatively between the behaviour of a man and that of a frog, may seem to have some support in the facts. One might, again, take psycho-analysis more seriously if it applied to the genuinely religious Buddha as perfectly as it does to the pseudo-religious Rousseau and his innumerable spiritual progeny. It is well therefore, if one does not wish to fall victim to the fallacies of the naturalist, to turn from an age like our own which tends to see in life only a free expansion of wonder and curiosity to certain periods of the past that were more preoccupied with the problem of religious or humanistic control. The situation with which Buddha had to cope in his affirmation of the principle of control was not so different from our own as one might infer from his remoteness in time and place. He lived in an age of extreme philosophical sophistication. Naturalistic doctrines were being proclaimed very similar in their practical implications to scientific determinism. One of these doctrines, especially subversive of moral responsibility, Buddha declared to be the worst of all, just, he added, as a hair garment is the worst of garments, hot in summer, cold in winter, uncomfortable at all seasons.

In general, there is an irreconcilable opposition between Buddhism and any philosophy or psychology ancient or modern, that tends, on any grounds whatsoever, to obscure the truths of the higher will. Buddha's emphasis on this will is so fundamental that, according to a German authority, his teaching may be summed up in the lines of Goethe :

> Von der Gewalt die alle Menschen bindet
> Befreit der Mensch sich der sich überwindet —

lines that recall a sentence of Milton's : 'He who reigns within himself and rules passions, desires and fears, is more than a king.' One should not forget, however, that, though Buddhism is hostile to all doctrines that deny a principle of control in human nature, it is not necessarily in accord with every doctrine that affirms such a principle. The sayings of Goethe and Milton I have just quoted would have met the approval of a Stoic. Milton's use of the word king is indeed very much in the Stoical tradition. Yet the wisdom of Buddha, whatever it may be, is not, as I have already remarked, Stoical. One needs to keep in mind here the ordinary contrast between Stoic pride and Christian humility, for the same contrast exists between the Stoic and the Buddhist. The source of Stoical pride would seem to be an usurpation on the part of reason of a primacy that does not belong to it, with a resulting attempt to bring all the facts of experience under a single law, the law of 'nature.' The Stoic thus comes to deny dualism in his metaphysical theory at the same time that he asserts it in his ethical practice. In other words, he seeks to base the principle of control on a philosophy of immanence ; whereas both Christianity and Buddhism are, though on different postulates, transcendent. Everything will be found to hinge finally on the idea of meditation. This idea has suffered a steady decline in the Occident, along with the transcendent view of life in general, in the passage from the mediaeval to the modern period. Yet it is not certain that religion itself can survive unless men retain some sense of the wisdom that may, according to Dante, be won by sitting in quiet recollection. The meditation of the Buddhist involves like that of the Christian the exercise of transcendent will ; this will is not, however, associated, as it normally is in the meditation of the Christian, with that of a personal deity. Persons of positive and critical temper who yet perceive the importance of meditation may incline here as elsewhere to put less emphasis on the doctrinal divergence of Christianity and Buddhism than on their psychological agreement.

INDEX OF NAMES